FOLKESTONE
A Pictorial History

FOLKESTONE
A Pictorial History

Charles E. Whitney

Photographs from the collections of
EAMONN ROONEY, ALAN TAYLOR
and **ROY WILSON**

Phillimore

1986

Published by
PHILLIMORE & CO. LTD.
Shopwyke Hall, Chichester, Sussex

ISBN 0 85033 596 5

Printed and bound in Great Britain by
BIDDLES LTD.
Guildford, Surrey

For my parents, Edward and Margaret Whitney,
who like many before them visited Folkestone,
liked it – and stayed.

Contents

I	General Views
II	Sandgate
III	Cheriton
IV	Foord
V	Folkestone Harbour, Fishmarket and Stade
VI	Streets and Trades
VII	The Leas
VIII	The Beach along Lower Sandgate Road
IX	Other Places of Recreation
X	Churches and Chapels
XI	East Cliff and the Warren
XII	Other Glimpses of Bygone Folkestone
XIII	The First World War
XIV	Between the Wars and Floral Folkestone

List of Illustrations

1. Late 17th-century map of Folkestone
2. Engraving of Folkestone, c.1790
3. Early 19th-century engraving of the town and harbour
4. Engraving of the stade, c.1840
5. The stade area and Cubitt's viaduct
6. Plan of Folkestone, 1874

Sandgate

7. Sandgate Castle, c.1735
8. John Gough's cottage, Sandgate
9. The turnpike toll, Sandgate
10. View from the Leas, 1870s
11. Sandgate High Street, 1877
12. Sandgate High Street, 1887
13. St Paul's, Sandgate
14. Parish church, Sandgate
15. Sandgate Hill Lift
16. James Morris
17. Sandgate seafront, 1899
18. Sandgate High Street, c.1900
19. The 'Toast Rack', c.1901
20. Seabrook in Sandgate station
21. Peace parade, 1919

Cheriton

22. All Soul's church, Cheriton
23. Shaftesbury Avenue, Cheriton
24. Sanitary Steam Laundry, Cheriton
25. Cheriton Electric Hall, 1911
26. Cheriton High Street, 1911
27. View towards Newington, c.1910
28. Grounds of St Martin's Rectory, 1909
29. St Martin's, Cheriton

Foord

30. Mid-19th-century etching of Chalybeate Well
31. Engraving of Foord and viaduct, 1844
32. The viaduct, 1865

33. The *Black Bull* public house
34. After the flood of 1909

Folkestone Harbour, Fishmarket and Stade

35. Folkestone harbour, 1858
36. Folkestone harbour, c.1890
37. Folkestone harbour, c.1896
38. The royal train, 1899
39. The new pier promenade,
40. The *Duchess of York*, c.1898
41. Harbour quay, c.1908
42. One of Smith's ice carts
43. Folkestone harbour's 'marine porters'
44. Fishing luggers, c.1880
45. The tan house, c.1911
46. Folkestone fishmarket, c.1906
47. Folkestone's fishermen's band, c.1900
48. Folkestone fishmarket, c.1910
49. Harvest festival at the fishermen's Bethel
50. Fishermen clearing mackerel nets
51. The Blessing of the Fisheries, 1927
52. The old fishing quarter, 1934
53. The harbour waterfront, Folkestone, 1935

Streets and Trades

54. The Cistern House
55. Sandgate Road, c.1862
56. Sandgate Road, 1900s
57. Sherwood & Son, Sandgate Road
58. Carlo Maestrani's restaurant, Sandgate Road
59. Staff of the restaurant, 1908
60. Guildhall Street, early 1900s
61. Guildhall Street between 1907 and 1914
62. Rendezvous Street, c.1914
63. Messrs. Cave, Edwards & Co., early 1900s
64. The old High Street, early 1900s
65. Richard Hart, coal merchant, c.1911
66. Morley's butcher's shop, Dover Road
67. J. W. Cann's motor transport firm

68. Winners of the Westbrook Challenge Shield for fire-fighting, 1908
69. Dawson's Mill, Cheriton Road
70. Morehall post office, Cheriton Road, c.1908
71. Shop at No.14 Bouverie Road West
72. The *King's Arms*, c.1875
73. The *Belle-Vue* Hotel, St John's Street
74. The *Bouverie Arms*, c.1859
75. The *Royal Pavilion Hotel* in the 1900s
76. The *Westcliff Hotel*, 1904

The Leas

77. View of the Leas, early 1880s
78. View of the Leas from the west, early 1990s
79. The Metropole Lift
80. The upper Leas and Madeira Walk, c.1918
81. Statue of William Harvey, c.1905
82. The old Leas Shelter, c.1905
83. The Leas Cliff Hall, c.1927
84. An original mode of transport
85. Llama and trap, 1930s
86. The Leas Bandstand, c.1915
87. Folkestone's second lift, 1902
88. The front of the Leas Pavilion
89. Interior of the Leas Pavilion Tea Rooms
90. Folkestone harbour from the Leas, 1910
91. The Tudor gun on the Leas, c.1914
92. Albert Burvill, policeman for the Earl of Radnor

The Beach along Lower Sandgate Road

93. Folkestone Gas Works, c.1860
94. Folkestone's Bathing Establishment
95. Fagg's bathing carriages
96. Advertisement from 1896/7 Pike's Directory for the Folkestone Bathing Establishment
97. The Victoria Pier
98. Folkestone lifeboat station
99. The switchback railway
100. On the switch back, c.1910
101. Pleasure-boat men, 1930s
102. Folkestone Regatta Day, c.1900

Other Places of Recreation

103. Radnor Park, c.1896
104. The Bayle Pond, c.1900
105. Frank Funnell's four-horse coach service, early 20th century
106. The 'Active' coach time-table
107. Handbill for Boxing Night, 1887
108. Advertisement for the *East Kent Arms*, early 1900s

109. The Pleasure Gardens Theatre
110. Theatre publicity, 1897
111. Prices for theatre admission
112. The Pleasure Gardens, c.1915
113. Aerial view of the Pleasure Gardens, 1925
114. The Art Treasures Exhibition, 1886
115. Military tournament, 1905
116. The Central Picture Theatre, c.1915
117. Coronation film invitation, 1911
118. Advertisement for Benefit Concert, 1893

Churches and Chapels

119. Statue of St Eanswythe
120. Interior of the parish church, c.1850
121. Exterior of the parish church, c.1850
122. The parish church, c.1864
123. The parish church, c.1885
124. Interior of Christ Church, Sandgate Road, 1905
125. Christ Church, c.1870
126. St Michael's church, Dover Road
127. Interior of St Michael's church, c.1904
128. The Congregational church, Tontine Street
129. The Wesleyan Methodist church

East Cliff and the Warren

130. The old *Warren Inn*, East Cliff, c.1880
131. Copt Point, East Cliff, c.1910
132. Warren Halt, c.1914
133. Loading hay on East Cliff, 1920s
134. Roman site looking south
135. Roman site, main corridor and rooms adjoining
136. View across East Cliff, 1920s
137. East Cliff between the wars

Other Glimpses of Bygone Folkestone

138. Funeral service, 1878
139. The drinking fountain, Kingsbridge Street
140. The Royal Victoria Hospital, early 1900s
141. Sgt. Albert Ames of the 'Buffs'
142. Long-service certificate
143. The mayor and corporation, 1909
144. Edward Sassoon's election campaign
145. The Holy Trinity cricket team, 1913
146. Polling Day, 1910
147. The proclamation of George V, 1910

The First World War

148. Moritz Worms
149. German prisoners, 1914
150. Austrian prisoners, 1914

151. Cavalry on parade at Shorncliffe Camp, 1914
152. Belgian soldiers, 1914
153. Some of the craft used for Belgian refugees in 1914
154. Departure of Belgian soldiers, Folkestone Pier
155. Verse by J. Anderson
156. Sir Stephen Penfold at the parish church, 1915
157. King George V at Cheriton, 1915
158. Potato queue, Cheriton, 1916
159. School certificate, 1917
160. 'Gebby', the fund raiser
161. First World War postcard
162. The Manor House on the Leas, 1917
163. Folkestone Big Gun Week, 1918
164. Billet form, 1917
165. Rest camp, Marine Parade

Between the Wars and Floral Folkestone

166. German U-boat, 1919
167. Peace tea, 1919
168. World War One tank, 1919
169. War memorial on the Leas
170. The Prince of Wales, Royal Victoria Hospital, 1921
171. Opening of the Leas Cliff Hall, 1927
172. Official programme for Prince Henry's visit, 1927
173. Items on the programme
174. Prince Henry passing the lifeboat *Leslie*
175. Folkestone Municipal Orchestra, 1928
176. The zig-zag path
177. Jubilee flower-bed on the Leas, 1935
178. Kingsnorth Gardens
179. Gardens, Lower Sandgate Road

Charles Whitney would like to acknowledge the use of the photographs and ephemera in this book as follows: **Eamonn Rooney** for nos. 1, 5, 7, 10, 13, 14, 16, 21, 22, 28, 36, 37, 38, 39, 40, 41, 50, 66, 78, 79, 80, 82, 83, 84, 85, 86, 87, 89, 90, 92, 100, 102, 106, 107, 110, 111, 112, 113, 117, 118, 119, 120, 121, 122, 124, 130, 131, 132, 135, 140, 144, 159, 171, 176, 178, 179; **Alan Taylor** for nos. 2, 4, 9, 12, 15, 17, 20, 23, 24, 25, 26, 27, 29, 31, 32, 33, 34, 35, 42, 43, 44, 45, 46, 47, 48, 49, 52, 54, 55, 57, 58, 59, 61, 63, 64, 65, 67, 68, 70, 71, 72, 73, 74, 76, 77, 81, 88, 91, 93, 96, 97, 98, 101, 103, 105, 108, 114, 115, 116, 123, 125, 129, 133, 137, 138, 139, 141, 142, 143, 145, 146, 147, 148, 149, 150, 151, 152, 153, 154, 155, 156, 157, 160, 161, 162, 163, 165, 166, 167, 168, 170, 172, 173, 174, 175, 177; **Roy Wilson** for nos. 3, 6, 8, 18, 19, 30, 53, 56, 60, 62, 69, 75, 94, 95, 99, 104, 109, 126, 127, 128, 134, 136, 158, 164, 169.

Acknowledgements

I should like to thank Brian Boreham and his colleagues at Folkestone's Reference Library for their unfailing courtesy and help when I asked some particularly obscure questions.

I have been more than fortunate to work with three such generous, friendly experts as Eamonn Rooney, Alan Taylor and Roy Wilson on this project. They spent innumerable evenings sifting through their vast collections of photographs, offering advice, providing information and making useful suggestions. No query was too trivial and seemingly no topic was outside their enthusiastic knowledge. If, unusually, they could not provide an answer, then they generally knew someone who could. To those others whose advice was sought, many of whom are members of Folkestone and District Local History Society, I am very grateful. I am also grateful to Alan's wife, Eileen, who provided much-needed cups of coffee and cheerfully put up with our protracted discussions in her sitting-room.

My wife and daughters bore the brunt of an absentee husband and father with understanding and resigned good humour when they were not providing hospitality for yet more meetings between Eamonn, Alan, Roy and myself. To them I give my very real thanks.

This book would never have seen the light of day without the friendly advice and persistence of Frances Mee of Phillimore's, whose understanding patience went far beyond the call of duty.

Finally, although care has been taken to eliminate errors, I apologise for any that should be discovered.

Introduction

No one can say when people first settled in or around Folkestone. The origin of the name has itself aroused controversy which has never been finally resolved. Judith Glover in *The Place Names of Kent* (1976) has suggested that it comes from Folca's Stone, a rock marking the meeting place of the local people, although who Folca was and where his stone was both remain mysteries. Dr. C. H. Bishop in *Folkestone, The Story of a Town* thinks it might be a 'Saxon adaptation of an ancient Celtic original', and could be connected with the pre-Roman British Prince Folgens. Even the spelling was not finally regulated until a 19th-century lord of the manor insisted on Folkestone being spelt as it is today.

Traces of Neolithic, Bronze Age and Iron Age man have been discovered in the area while evidence that Belgic invaders were present during the first century B.C. have been found at Cheriton and on the East Cliff. S. E. Winbolt's *Roman Folkestone* (1925) gives a detailed account of the extensive archaeological work that was done on a Roman villa discovered on East Cliff in 1924. The site was finally covered over in 1954 by the council. Roman Folkestone was not a key place in the province but it was en route between Dover (Portus Dubræ) and Lympne (Portus Lemanæ), both important ports, and the villa tiles and others found nearby suggest that it might have been the residence of a senior official of the *Classis Britannica* or soldiers serving with the Roman fleet although originally it was almost certainly the residence of a British landowner.

The departure of the Romans towards the end of the fourth century A.D. and the advent of the Anglo-Saxon invasions which were to continue over the next century or two, brought Saxon and especially Jutish peoples to this part of England. In 1907, a Jutish burial ground was found close to the main road on Dover Hill.

The Kingdom of Kent was established during the sixth century, being one of the heptarchy, or seven Anglo-Saxon Kingdoms in England. St Augustine's mission to Kent in 598 and the baptism of King Æthelbert *c.*599 were to have consequences for Folkestone, for Æthelbert's son, Eadbald, who became king in 616, reluctantly allowed Eanswythe, his daughter, to set up a community at Folkestone around 630. He may well have been influenced in his decision by the knowledge that he had just completed a fortress or *ballium*, probably consisting of earthern ramparts and wooden palisades, close by the site of the proposed nunnery. Eanswythe was extremely young – possibly just sixteen – when she became Abbess. It is to Capgrave, quoted in Bollandist's *Acta Sanctorium* (1868) and refered to in Dame Eanswythe Edwards's *St. Eanswythe of Folkestone* (1983) that we owe accounts of miracles attributed to the saint, notably a wooden beam extending itself in answer to prayer and the restoration of sight to a blind woman. It was also claimed that she made water run uphill but this probably had more to do with the ingenious use of aqueducts to bring fresh water from the Castle Hill area to the nunnery rather than to any supernatural phenomenon. Reports suggest that she showed 'motherly solicitude' for her nuns. Tradition has it that she died in 640, probably at the age of 26. Her church did not survive long after her. The eroding sea may have taken its toll or perhaps it was a fierce attack by the Vikings in 867 which finally destroyed the nunnery. What is clear is that the nuns transferred the relics of St Eanswythe to the nearby church of SS Peter and Paul.

In 927 King Athelstan granted the remaining land on which the community had been situated to the monks of Christchurch, Canterbury. They set about re-establishing a community, this time for men. In 1052, Earl Godwin, banished from the court of King Edward the Confessor for challenging his authority, raided Folkestone and destroyed it and the monastery on his way up to London, where he became once more arguably the most powerful man in England.

The Norman Conquest in 1066 brought a new social and political order which resulted in King William's half-brother, Bishop Odo of Bayeux, becoming Earl of Kent and lord of the manor of Folkestone. It was not long before Odo, in his greed, over-reached himself and was duly disgraced. Another Norman, William D'Arcy, became lord of the manor. He probably built some kind of wooden fortification either on what is now called the Bayle or Castle Hill. The Domesday Survey was completed at about the same time, in 1086. It was D'Arcy's brother-in-law, Nigel de Muneville, who, succeeding to the lordship of the manor, built a new church and priory for Folkestone in 1095. Unfortunately, this too eventually became unsafe as the cliff gradually disappeared into the sea.

A third lord of the manor, William d'Averanches, a descendant of Nigel de Muneville, founded what was eventually to become the present parish church as well as a priory. The church was dedicated to SS Mary and Eanswythe. The relics of the latter were said to have been translated to this new church in 1138, on 12 September, which in subsequent years has always been kept as the patronal festival. The Benedictine monks, who had stayed since 1095, were to continue their community with mixed fortune until the dissolution of the monasteries in 1535.

The Folkestone population consisted of 209 villagers and 83 smallholders at the time of the Domesday Survey in 1086, when Folkestone was worth £100. To the south lay Hythe and to the north Dover, both of them head ports of the Confederation of Cinque Ports, although neither had a population greater than 1,200 by 1300. King Stephen granted Folkestone some taxation privileges during the mid-12th century, although why is not clear. It was not until 1205 that Folkestone was granted the right to hold a market every Thursday, a right confirmed in a charter of 1215. Subsequently, Folkestone gained the right to a Tuesday fair from 1349 and in 1390 a Wednesday market was also granted. With these privileges, Folkestone was beginning to acquire the status of a small town. The community's farming and fishing industries together with a significant quarrying trade all contributed to Folkestone's economy. One of the quarries, belonging to the lord of the manor, sent 4,000 stone cannon balls to Calais in 1351. Folkestone stone was used for Sheppey Castle and Wye church. Yet another factor may have been that St Eanswythe's relics were, as Dame Eanswythe Edwards points out, '... a great object of pilgrimage in the Middle Ages'. The pilgrims would obviously have brought additional trade to the locality.

Occasionally, Folkestone played a brief role on the national stage. In 1213, King John used the town as his headquarters when he negotiated with Pandulph, the Papal Legate, over who should be the next Archbishop of Canterbury. Unless the Pope had his way, Pandulph threatened that King Philip Augustus of France would be authorised to invade England in the Pope's name. John succumbed to the demands, even accepting the Pope as his overlord. A frustrated Philip Augustus was now forbidden to invade but this did not stop him raiding the south-east coast of England in 1216, in which he burned both Folkestone and its church.

In 1313 King Edward II granted the town a Charter of Incorporation, by which it could elect a mayor, bailiff and 12 jurats. It was also at about this time that Folkestone joined the Cinque Ports as a 'Corporate Limb' of Dover. The Cinque Ports had gradually developed from before the Norman Conquest. In return for supplying ships and men to the monarch for an agreed number of days each year, he bestowed rights and privileges on the principal ports involved: Sandwich, Dover, Hythe, New Romney and Hastings and later Rye and Winchelsea. Other settlements on the coast wanted to be part of this useful deal, and so the more important were allowed to become 'Corporate Limbs' of the Head Ports. Smaller communities became 'Non-corporate Limbs'. The system, when later set out in Charles II's Charter of 1668, showed seven Head Ports, seven Corporate Limbs and 24 Non-corporate Limbs. Edward I appointed a Lord Warden in 1278 to keep an eye on what was happening. Today it is little more than a sinecure, although a great honour, in the gift of the monarch. Sir Winston Churchill, Sir Robert Menzies and Queen Elizabeth the Queen Mother are three recent, distinguished holders of the office. However, medieval Cinque Portsmen were no romantics. They were tough rogues. Their propensity to attack continental merchant shipping and 'confiscate' cargo resulted in the French, together with some sympathetic Scots, pillaging and burning Folkestone in 1378 as a reprisal.

The Tudor period saw Folkestone with a population of about five hundred. Henry VIII, through sanctioning Thomas Cromwell's ideas about the dissolution of the monasteries, brought about the closure of Folkestone Priory in 1535 which by then consisted of just the prior, Thomas Bassett, and one old, sick monk. Thomas Bassett's efforts at keeping the priory open by adding the prior's common seal to the Acknowledgement of Supremacy in 1534 had not been enough. The document and the seal are still kept in the chapter house of Westminster Abbey. Henry VIII was aware that his break with the Roman Catholic Church and confiscation of its property made it more likely that France or Spain might invade. With the sale of Church lands and possessions he commissioned several shore forts to be built, one being Sandgate Castle, standing just outside Folkestone to the south. It was completed in 1539, taking just 18 months to build. Henry certainly visited it, possibly during his visit to Folkestone in 1542, when he came to discuss the possibility of creating a harbour. It is not known whether he made an offer to the town, or if his offer was refused, but no harbour resulted from the negotiations. Meanwhile, in addition to the castle being built, at least one gun was sited on the Bayle, trenches were dug both there and on East Cliff and bows and arrows purchased. Thomas Cromwell, briefly Earl of Essex and from 1531 to 1542 Secretary of State to Henry, was lord of the manor of Folkestone prior to his arrest and execution in 1542.

In 1545, towards the end of Henry VIII's reign, 24 councillors were added to the corporation of Folkestone. The mayor was elected every year on 8 September at the cross in the churchyard. Every freeman was entitled to vote and was awarded 6d. (2½p) when he did so. However, Tudor Folkestone was not just concerned with matters national and political. Townsfolk enjoyed being entertained. O. B. Grover's article 'Tudor Folkestone' in *Folkestone Past and Present* (1954), edited by R. J. Howarth, notes that during the 1540s the then mayor of Folkestone, Thomas Hunt, bought '... a bear and a garden for £4'. Bear-baiting was both common and popular. The King's 'bereward' even came. The King's jester, the Earl of Hertford's minstrels and other entertainers also visited.

Elizabeth I's reign also proved an anxious time for England, especially after the execution of the Roman Catholic Mary Queen of Scots in February 1587. It was hardly suprising, then, that Folkestone contributed boats to the Cinque Ports fleet and recruited and trained men for the county militia, as well as mounting guns on the cliffs as its part in the country's defences when the Spanish Armada of King Philip II attempted to invade in 1588.

It was during Elizabeth's reign that Folkestone's most famous son was born in a house off Mercery Lane, now Church Street, on 1 April 1578. William Harvey, whose father, Thomas, served as mayor four times, was educated at King's School, Canterbury, and went up to Caius College, Cambridge, in 1593. He stayed there six years studying medicine and subsequently went to the University of Padua, receiving his doctorate in 1602 before returning to Cambridge to gain his M.D. He was appointed physician to St Bartholomew's Hospital, London, in 1609 and it was not long before he was lecturing on topics concerning the circulation of the blood. He published books on the subject in 1628 and 1651. He became physician to James I in 1618 and to Charles I in 1631. He is considered to be one of the first to have used scientific method in medicine and was a pioneer in embryology and a founder of gynaecology. He was the first Englishman to write on midwifery. He built a hall and library for the College of Physicians, who elected him president in 1654. However, he declined the honour on account of his old age. He died in 1657. A statue to him by A. B. Joy stands on the Leas and was unveiled in 1881, while a few years earlier, in 1874, C. E. Knight's west window of the parish church was donated by the medical profession as a memorial to him. The great man bequeathed £200 to Folkestone, a considerable sum in those days. Partly through that and partly through his brother Eliab's will and his nephew Sir Eliab Harvey's determination, a Folkestone school was founded in 1674, which is known today as the Harvey Grammar School. Such a school was badly needed – Folkestone's first recorded schoolmaster was not appointed until 1564 and he did not stay long.

In the Civil War, Folkestone and the surrounding area was parliamentarian in its sympathies, although Folkestone fishermen may have regretted that not only because it was during Charles I's reign that they received permission to erect jetties from the stade – a first, tentative move towards a harbour – but also because Cromwell's Commonwealth brought in a law forbidding swearing in 1651 and many fishermen were heavily fined. In 1654, John Digby, the Earl of Bristol's son, was arrested as he attempted to slip across the channel. However, as soon as Charles II returned as king in 1660, the town was quick to replace with royalists officials who had had parliamentarian sympathies. In 1665 the plague also returned, having visited Folkestone previously in 1624.

In 1697 Jacob des Bouverie bought the lordship of the manor. He was descended from Lawrence des Bouverie who, coming to Britain from Flanders in the 16th century, settled in Canterbury. Jacob had connections with merchants from London and his eldest son, Edward, was a successful merchant who was knighted by James II. In 1765 they were created Earls of Radnor, the eldest son becoming Viscount Folkestone until succeeding to the Earldom. The des Bouverie association with

Folkestone is clear from the names of roads and squares, such as Earls Avenue, Bouverie Square, Bouverie Road and Radnor Park.

Folkestone's fortunes seem to have improved during the course of the 18th century. Daniel Defoe in his *Journey Through England* (1725) commented: 'From Dover along the sea coast I passed a miserable fishing town, called Folkestone, miserable in its appearance'. However, it was calculated that in 1729 there were 450 houses and 2,000 inhabitants, making it three times the size of the Tudor town. Perhaps the great outbreak of smallpox in 1720 which claimed 145 victims had contributed to the town's unattractiveness. Smallpox was to strike badly again in 1765 with 158 people dying. On the other hand, perhaps C. Seymour's *Survey of the Cities, Towns and Villages of the County of Kent* (1776) was rather over-optimistic when the author described Folkestone as being 'wealthy and populous' and commented on the large size of the fishing fleet. Three attempts had already been made to do something about the erosion and deterioration of the stade in 1635, 1654 and 1709, but it would be at least another century before the problem was properly tackled.

The 18th century also saw the rise of nonconformity in Folkestone. The Baptists first arrived in 1698, their meeting house finally being built in 1729. The Quakers were certainly in Folkestone by 1684 and had built a new meeting house by 1790. Congregationalists were established in Folkestone in 1797 although Wesleyan Methodists did not form a group until 1824.

The greater tolerance in matters religious occurred at a time when there was also growth in smuggling, or 'Owling' as it was called. S. J. Mackie, a Victorian local historian, in his *Folkestone and its Neighbourhood* and *Gleanings from the Municipal Records* (1883) notes that the first Folkestone smuggling records refer to wool being smuggled to France in 1696, although it had probably been occurring before that. Increasingly, wines, tobacco, silks and general luxury items were smuggled from the continent. Coastguards, preventive officers and dragoons were stationed along this coast to enforce the law and although they had their successes they did not make much impression on the local population, most of whom were in the smugglers' confidence. C. H. Bishop's 'The Langhornes' in *Some Folkestone Worthies* underlines this: he notes that the Revd. William Langhorne, vicar of Folkestone 1754-72, '... preached against smuggling, but ... popular opinion in the town obliged him to desist'. L. R. Jones, in his article 'Smuggling Days in Folkestone' in *Folkestone Past and Present* (1954), quotes Captain Joseph Cockburn, who gave evidence before a Royal Commission in 1746. 'He had been a smuggler and was for long a figure in the "trade". He stated that at least six tons of tea and 2,000 half-ankers [5 gallons] of brandy were imported every week from Boulogne, six cutters being used for the purpose.' The coastline from Margate to Romney Marsh was a hotbed of smuggling which was probably at its height during the first half of the 19th century. In 1819 a brig, the *Pelter*, was stationed at the Warren as a headquarters for preventive officers, since smuggling activity had been increased with the advent of guinea smuggling. Rothschilds, the merchant bankers, were supplying soldiers in the Peninsular War with their pay, but it had to be ferried across the channel discreetly. This was achieved by Folkestone smugglers, who had special galleys of 12 oars built to take the gold, which might be worth anything up to £30,000 on any one shipment.

However, smuggling craft were lost and widows and children became dependent on the parish. Smugglers were also caught. Five Folkestone men were sentenced in London in 1750; three more from Maidstone were transported in 1820. In January

1823 a ship, the *Four Brothers*, set sail from Flushing for Folkestone with a crew of 26 and about £10,000 worth of contraband goods aboard. Intercepted by the *Badger*, a preventive cutter, some miles off Dungeness, there followed a gun battle. Four smugglers were killed, six injured and the survivors faced a charge of firing at a king's ship. Fortunately, as the defence showed, the offending ship was Dutch and most of the crew were Dutch-born, an interesting sidelight on Folkestone life as some expectant mothers of the town deliberately went over to Holland to have their children to protect them from the press-gangs which were quite common. The defendants were acquitted and returned to a heroes' welcome in Folkestone. There was also strong community loyalty. On 26 May 1820, 11 Folkestone men were caught smuggling and put in Dover gaol. A large mob set off from Folkestone and, arriving in Dover, saw that the prison, just off Market Square, already had a large crowd of Dover men around it. Sir Thomas Mantel, Dover's mayor, attempted to read the Riot Act, but it was torn from his hand. Captain McCulloch, in charge of some hastily-summoned soldiers from Dover Castle, refused to fire on the crowd. The prisoners were abducted, their manacles removed and they were carried off to Folkestone to be set free. They were never retaken, even though rewards of up to £100, a considerable sum in those days, were offered by the Dover authorities.

However, it must not be thought that the early days of the 19th century were totally given over to smuggling. Another preoccupation was Napoleon's threatened invasion. Lists were prepared, the local population donated £150 14s. 0d. towards the cost of local defence while the Earl of Radnor contributed a further £100. It was also decided to raise two companies of volunteers. Martello Towers were built. The idea came from a similar building which held up an eventually successful British military action at Mortella Point, part of the defences of the Gulf of San Fiorenco, Corsica, during the latter part of the 18th century. Some years later, Captain W. H. Ford, R.E., suggested that a chain of towers built along the lines of the Corsican one should be built to defend the coast. Construction was begun in 1805 and was completed in 1808-9. Towers were built from Folkestone's East Cliff round to Seaford, Sussex. Others were built along the coastline of Essex and Suffolk. The first three were constructed to protect East Wear Bay and Folkestone harbour while the fourth was part of the defences of Shorncliffe Camp from its position at the west end of the Leas. The traversing cannon on top of each tower weighed about two-and-a-half tons and fired a 24 pound shot. Each tower could accommodate an officer and 24 men.

A second factor in the defence of Folkestone at this time was the opening of Shorncliffe Army Camp in 1794 on 229 acres which the government had bought a year or two earlier. It was at Shorncliffe in 1803 that Sir John Moore assumed command of the brigade that he was to take to the Iberian Peninsula and to his last battle at Corunna. The Royal Military Canal at Hythe, also part of the defence arrangements, was built between 1805 and 1809. Nevertheless, all these preparations were not needed as Napoleon never came.

While Folkestone was maintaining its notoriety as a centre of smuggling and was preparing to defend itself against Napoleon, other forces were at work. In 1795, sea-bathing from bathing machines at Folkestone was being advertised in the *Kentish Gazette* for the first time, a somewhat belated attempt to catch up with other towns along the south and south-east coasts which were already becoming resorts. Brighton in Sussex had been a popular resort since about 1750; Margate had been developing a similar role·in Kent from around 1765. The rising expectations of visitors may have been a factor in the passing of a private Act of Parliament in March 1796 '... for paving, repairing and cleansing the Highways, Streets and Lanes, in the Town of Folkestone'. There was much to do. Commissioners of Paving ordered roads to be drained, widened and, unfortunately, renamed. Mercery Lane became Church Street, Fisherman's Row was changed to Radnor Street, Gulston Street became South Street and so on. There were later changes, too, the best-known being the gradual change of Cow Street into a more extended Sandgate Road. Shellons Lane became Guildhall Street. Virtually non-existent sanitation was considerably improved until Dr. W. Bateman could assure the Association of Public Sanitary Inspectors meeting in Folkestone in September 1889 that 'the streets are swept every day and I think it would be difficult to find a cleaner town'. However, that was in the future. In 1830, changes were so slow that there was still little to induce people to stay at Folkestone and too few lodging houses anyway.

Apart from the efforts of the Commissioners of Paving, three inter-related major factors helped transform the small, rather squalid town of 1830 into a fashionable resort and busy cross-channel port by the end of the century.

The first and most important factor was the coming of the railway direct from London. It was finally opened on 28 June 1843. The line down to the harbour was in use early in 1844, its main task originally being to bring seaborne coal up to the coke ovens at the junction station. The link to Dover was completed the same year. The outstanding feature of the railway at Folkestone is the huge Foord Viaduct, designed by William Cubitt, consisting of several million locally-made bricks.

The second key factor was the South-Eastern Railway Company's takeover of Folkestone harbour. By the beginning of the 19th century it had been finally realised that a large stone-built harbour would have to be constructed, not just a stone pier or landing stage. Accordingly, a Folkestone Harbour Company had been set up in 1807, which went bankrupt in 1842. Seizing the opportunity, the South-Eastern Railway Company bought the harbour for a reasonable £18,000 in 1843. Thus train services could now be tied in with boat sailings. The result was an early appreciation of the possibilities of comparatively swift travel to the continent which quickly led to greater trade for Folkestone and the development of the harbour, culminating in the final extension of the pier whose last stone was laid by the French Ambassador on 12 July 1904.

The third major factor was the decision by the Earl of Radnor to develop Folkestone. In this he was following a trend already set by other noble landowners at Bournemouth, Eastbourne and elsewhere. Lord Radnor chose Sidney Smirke, a London architect, to develop the Folkestone estate. Initially, they thought that the town would expand eastwards, and schemes were prepared which took account of that but it quickly became clear that demand was towards the west. Wide, tree-lined streets were laid out, squares planned and, on land which had been formerly used for grazing, the Leas was created.

Those three major factors – the coming of the railway, and the development of both the harbour and the town – resulted in considerable population growth. In 1841 the population had been 4,413. Within 20 years, the population had virtually doubled to 8,507. By 1881 it had more than doubled again to 18,822. It was during this rapid period of expansion that photography first appeared, the earliest example in this volume dating from 1855. Coincidentally, that was the year that Charles

Dickens stayed at Albion Villas on the Leas for three months, writing very favourably about 'Pavilionstone', as he called the town, in his magazine *Out of Town*.

If the population expanded rapidly, the same was true of key buildings constructed around the town during this period. The first was the *Pavilion Hotel*, later the *Royal Pavilion Hotel*, built by the South-Eastern Railway Company in 1843 in order to improve the facilities available to cross-channel passengers. Such was its prestige that there were a number of letters about it in *The Times* during the century. The *Westcliff Hotel* (the *Majestic*) followed in 1856 and a new town hall was completed in 1861. Christ Church had been consecrated in 1850 but within the next 50 years five further churches, Holy Trinity, St John's, St Michael's, St Peter's and St Saviour's were also built as well as nonconformist and Roman Catholic places of worship. Hotels like the *Metropole* and the *Grand* were built to rival the *Royal Pavilion*. The Bathing Establishment, the Pleasure Gardens Theatre, the Victoria Pier, the Leas Shelter and the Radnor Club were all opened to cater for visitors. Services like gas, electricity and the telephone were also established.

In the Edwardian era, Folkestone reached its fashionable height with Herr Worms playing and conducting his band at various venues, the wealthy with their servants, carriages and bathchairs 'taking the air' on the Leas, while the Earl of Radnor's policeman ensured that 'socially undesirable' people kept well away. All this was to be cut short by the outbreak of the First World War in 1914. Soon after their country had been overrun, the first of 65,000 Belgian refugees began arriving, often possessing nothing except the clothes in which they stood. They were cared for by the Folkestone townspeople and the Belgian Committee for Refugees. From March 1915 onwards, Folkestone also became the main embarkation point for soldiers on their way to the fighting on the continent. Tens of thousands marched down to the harbour along what is now called the Road of Remembrance. Thousands of them returned, wounded, to the hastily-set-up hospitals, convalescent homes and rest camps that were opened in Folkestone. The town itself suffered an air raid on 25 May 1917, a bomb falling on crowded Tontine Street and causing 71 deaths and injury to ninety-six.

Peace came in 1918. Folkestone realised that it would not survive if it continued to concentrate on the more exclusive end of the holiday market, and so it broadened its appeal and tried to make itself generally more inviting by assuming the slogan 'Floral Folkestone'. Attractive flower-beds were laid out in Sandgate Road, the Leas, Radnor Park and elsewhere.

It was also during this period between the wars that Sandgate, which had had a separate Urban District Council since 1850, and Cheriton, which had had an Urban District Council since 1898, were absorbed into the Borough of Folkestone in 1934. Foord, which had sought a little fame as a possible spa, was swallowed up by Folkestone's expansion long before the turn of the century.

Here the pictorial history ends. Most of the photographs taken during the Second World War, when 35,000 people were evacuated, there were 77 air raids and six V-1s fell on the town, were published in *Frontline Folkestone* by the *Folkestone Herald* just after the war. Modern Folkestone can still be seen by visitors and residents alike. It is to be hoped that this history will not just entertain but will give the reader a clearer idea of how old Folkestone used to be, and will also stimulate others to further research.

The Plates

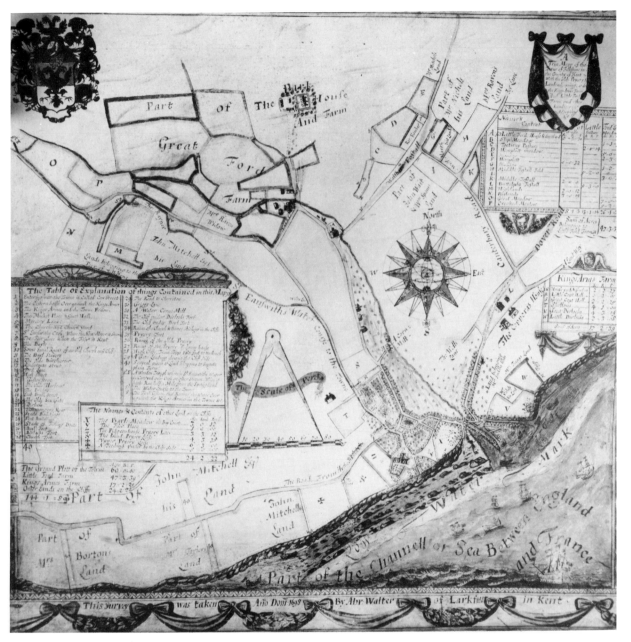

1. This map was prepared by Abraham Walter of Larkfield within a year of Jacob des Bouverie acquiring the lordship of the manor of Folkestone in 1697. It shows the coat of arms of the family in the top left hand corner. The town itself is found just to the right of the compass, and consisted of less than a dozen streets. The road from Hythe, a part of which was called Cow Street, later became Sandgate Road. Mercery Lane is today's Church Street while the Pent Stream played a larger part in the landscape than it does now. Note, too, the meadow up by the Bayle.

2. This is the earliest-known engraving of the town and dates from 1790. It comes from Edward Hasted's *History of Kent*. Folkestone's population at this time was between 3,000 and 4,000. There was no formal harbour, but on the far left can be seen the remains of one effort to protect the west cliff and the parish church in the 18th century. The predominant occupation was fishing and smuggling was still prevalent. One or two advertisements offering elegant bathing machines at Folkestone appeared in the *Kentish Gazette* in 1787 and 1788, but not until the beginning of the 19th century was a modest attempt made to turn Folkestone into a resort for sea-bathing and sea-water tasting.

3. George Shepherd's picture of the town and harbour was engraved by S. Lacey between 1828 and 1830. The foundation stone for the pier had been laid in 1808 and by 1810 it had been completed, thus providing a haven of about 14 acres. Although Folkestone was beginning to establish itself as a resort, the town on the cliff-top and the fishing community on the stade were still very much apart.

4. David Cox's view of the stade engraved by J. Rogers *c*.1840. One of the last views of Folkestone before the arrival of the railway in 1843, it gives a good impression of the closeness of the fisherfolk's dwellings to each other. On the left can be seen boatbuilders' sheds, which disappeared when the *Royal Pavilion* was built.

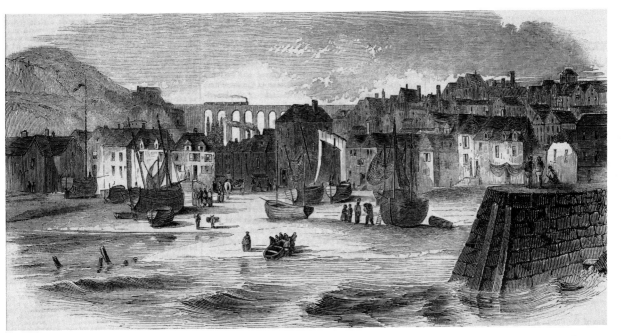

5. This shows the stade area complete with pier and, in the background, William Cubitt's impressive new viaduct consisting of several million locally-made bricks. It was built for the extension of the railway line to Dover, which opened in 1844. The branch line down to Folkestone harbour had yet to be built, passengers from the railway having to alight at Junction station and walk or take a horse-bus down to the harbour.

6. This plan of Folkestone comes from S. Mackie's *Handbook of Folkestone for Visitors 1874*. The shaded areas show where houses were being built at the time.

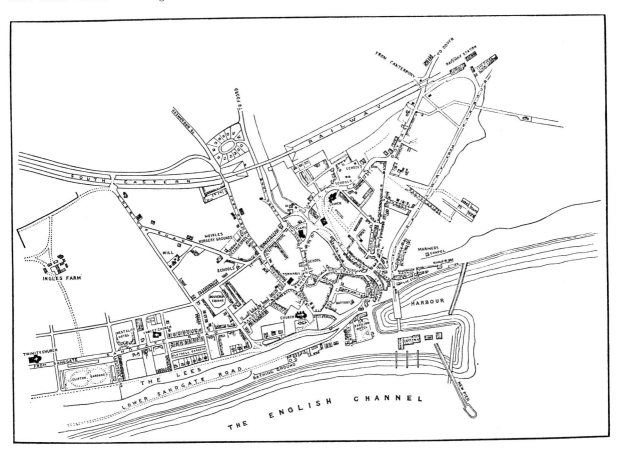

Sandgate

Sandgate seems to have had some reputation as a watering place towards the end of the 18th century. Some authorities credit Mr. Wilson, a shipbuilder, with having been the founder of the place. Although he built a few houses about the years 1770-80, according to Seymour's survey of 1776 there were already the beginnings of a settlement. Sandgate Castle was built on the orders of Henry VIII in 1539.

One of the main reasons for Sandgate's development, especially during the 19th century, was its close proximity to Shorncliffe army camp. Sandgate had its own Urban District Council from 1850 until 1934, when it was absorbed by the Borough of Folkestone.

7. Sandgate Castle was built in 1539 on the orders of Henry VIII who feared invasion from the continent. This print dates from 1735. As a shore fort, it was built to a similar plan to that of Camber and Deal castles, that is a central tower surrounded by semicircular bastions. The total cost was £2,887 14s. 0d. It was visited both by Henry VIII and by Elizabeth I. In the first years of the 19th century, a Martello Tower was superimposed on it. The castle continued to have a garrison until the 1880s.

8. This cottage, which stood near Sandgate Castle until 1883, was the birthplace of John B. Gough (1817-86), the well-known orator and champion of temperance. A soldiers' home in Sandgate High Street was named after him.

9. This photograph was taken just before the turnpike toll was abolished in 1877. It had existed from before 1780. The houses on the left are still there. The lady at the door is probably Mrs. Solley, the tollgate keeper's wife.

10. The view from the end of the Leas, looking over Sandgate, taken in about the mid-1870s. To the far right, marked by the line of houses, is the lane known today as Sandgate Hill. Almost as far to the right, the cow in the field marks the line of the old Sandgate Hill Lift. St Paul's, Sandgate, built in 1849, can be seen in the centre. Almost on the shore is Sandgate Castle with its Martello Tower in the middle. On the hilltop in the background, Shorncliffe Camp can just be seen.

11. This unusual and rather faded view of 1877 shows clearly the buildings clustered along the High Street, with the Castle behind. It is the only known photograph that shows a windmill being built to power a sawmill. However, within a year, high winds had blown the sails off.

12. This view, taken in about 1887, shows Sandgate High Street looking towards Hythe. The Fire Station on the extreme left was built in 1884, the Urban District Council's rooms being above. The little girl in white is looking in H. Longly's, which combined the trades of bicycle dealer, pianoforte teacher and music seller. On the right is Pear Tree Cottage while next to it is the building named after J. B. Gough, the temperance orator, known simply as the Soldiers' Home. It seems ironic that the building next to it should be H. & G. Simonds, a well-known local brewery.

13.   This photograph of St Paul's, Sandgate probably dates from the end of the last century. The galleries were not removed until 1915. The ones seen on the left were claimed by the Countess of Huntingdon, as well as a private entrance to the church, as it was her family's land on which the church had been built originally.

14.   In 1806 the Earl of Darnley purchased the Enbrook estate which stretched into Sandgate. In 1822 he built a small chapel on the edge of his property, on the site of the present church. Its most distinguished clergyman was the Revd. F. R. Nixon, who left in 1838, eventually becoming Bishop of Tasmania. In 1849 the church was rebuilt, much as it is seen today, the architect being S. S. Teulon (1812-73). The war memorial porch was added in 1919. The church was a chapel-of-ease until 1890, when it became a parish church in its own right.

15. (*above left*) The Sandgate Hill Lift opened in February 1893. It was over four times the length of the Leas Lifts. It passed the home of H. G. Wells, Spade House, by the bridge half-way up the track. The cost of repairs, the development of motor coaches and the First World War made the lift financially non-viable and the company dissolved in April 1924.

16. (*above right*) James Morris was born in 1795 into a banking family. He became a director of the Bank of England and from 1847-8 was its Governor. In 1852 he bought Encombe and he and his wife, Sophia, endowed Sandgate with a drinking fountain (1859), the National Schools (1866) and the James Morris Dwelling in the 1870s. He died in 1882.

17. (*below*) The sea was, and still is, a considerable problem to the west of Sandgate. This was what happened to the tram-track during a storm on 18 February 1899.

18. This view of Sandgate High Street, taken in about 1900, shows a variety of horse-drawn carriages awaiting hire, possibly from people alighting from the Sandgate Lift, opened in 1893 and just out of shot. The horse-drawn tram in the middle of the road ran from Sandgate to Hythe. This one was the all-weather variety, which offered some protection against the elements. The service began in 1891 and operated until 1921. The flagpole indicates the position of the *Royal Norfolk Hotel*, while just this side of it the Papillon Soldiers' Home, established in 1858, provided recreation for men from Shorncliffe Camp.

19.   Affectionately known as the 'Toast Rack', this was the summer version of the horse tram shown in plate 18. The service, begun in 1891, ran between the Sandgate schools, situated near the bottom of Sandgate Hill, and Red Lion Square, Hythe. The service ran every half hour and the fare for the whole distance of five miles in 1901, which is roughly when this picture was taken, was 3d. The service finally closed in 1921.

20. Seabrook in Sandgate station, situated west of the town in Seabrook, was the terminus of the South-Eastern Railway's single-track branch line from Sandling Junction down through Hythe. Prince Arthur, Duke of Connaught, cut the first sod in 1872. The line to Sandgate operated from 1874 to 1931. The truncated line to Hythe was completely closed in 1951.

21. Peace parades were common after the First World War, like this one in 1919. It is pictured as it was passing Simond's Brewery in the High Street.

Cheriton

The manor of Cheriton, which means a farmstead with, or by, a church, dates from ancient times. There is a passing reference to a church there in the late 11th century and it is referred to again during the reign of Edward I (1272-1307). The modern town dates from the 19th century and its prosperity was largely based on providing services for the army at Shorncliffe Camp, particularly laundry work. It also had its own live-stock market, which continued well into the present century. Cheriton Urban District Council existed from 1888 until 1934, when it was absorbed by the Borough of Folkestone.

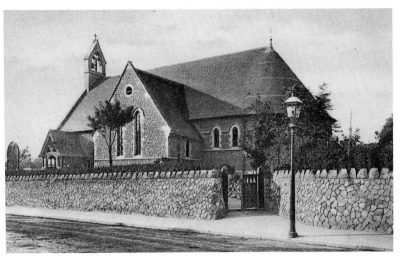

22. (*left*) All Souls' church, Cheriton, was built in 1893. Ewan Christian was the architect.

23. (*below*) Shaftesbury Avenue and, behind it, W. Martin's Ashley Mill, no longer working. The mill was originally built in Hythe in 1813, sold to Mr. Brissenden of Sandgate for £150 in 1875, taken down and re-erected in Cheriton and began work there in 1877. It was finally pulled down in 1919. To the right of the photograph can be seen the small Ashley Avenue Congregational church, which at that time was a branch of the main church at Tontine Street.

24. The scene inside No. 3 packing department at the Sanitary Steam Laundry, which was in Stanley Road, Cheriton and became Advance Laundries Ltd. during the 1930s. The sorting room processed 250,000 articles per week in 1924, somewhat later than when this photograph was taken. The laundry employed 150 workers and up to 180 at its busiest times.

25. Cheriton Electric Hall within weeks of its opening on 11 August 1911. It was situated on the corner of Cheriton High Street and Sydney Road, virtually next door to the *White Lion* public house. Inside, the cinema boasted 400 tip-up seats. During the First World War, it proved to be very popular with troops from Shorncliffe Camp. However, in 1923 it went out of business.

26. A view of Cheriton High Street and the Baptist church in about 1911.

27. Looking along what is now a main road out of Cheriton towards Newington in about 1910. Firs Farm is on the right.

28. This was the view in late 1909 onto grounds at least partly owned by St Martin's Rectory. It has since been developed. Horn Street Church of England Elementary School is in the foreground.

29. St Martin's was the original parish church of Cheriton, parts of which date from the Saxon and Norman periods Samuel Plimsoll, of Plimsoll line fame, lies buried in the graveyard.

Foord

Foord was a tiny hamlet just outside Folkestone, where the Pent Stream could be crossed. Glover notes a reference to it as Fforde as early as 1357. Once the railway had arrived and Folkestone expanded rapidly, which it did from 1843 onwards, Foord lost its separate identity.

30.   First referred to by Seymour in 1776 in his *Survey of Kent*, Chalybeate Spring water was held to have excellent health-giving properties. The 'notice' advertising the 'well' can be seen slightly to the right of centre of H. Stock's etching which dates from around 1850. Mr. J. G. Breach, of the *Pavilion Hotel*, had acquired it by the 1860s and built a ruined tower around it. In the 1860s a public house was opened opposite the site called the *Castle*. It was presumably named after the ruined tower. The spring has long since disappeared.

31. This engraving of Foord and its viaduct dates from 1844, when the viaduct had just been completed. In front of it to the right can be seen Bradstone Windmill, which stood at the top of what is now Bellevue Street. There has been a mill on that site since at least 1769. Bradstone Watermill is on the extreme left of the engraving. It may have been on the site since the 17th century. C. P. Davies has suggested that one of the earliest Baptists, John Case, was a miller and that this was probably his mill. It continued to work until 1894. In the Second World War, the wheel was cut up for scrap.

32. In this photograph of 1865, the water supply comes from a pump. The windmill, seen in the engraving, had disappeared. The garden to the rear of Mr. Stace's house, the large residence top right in the photograph, had become a Baptist cemetery. The Pent Stream now went under a culvert. The building in the right foreground was not demolished until 1972.

33. The *Black Bull* public house was situated rather out in the country and was not really a part of Foord or Folkestone. Opinions vary as to when it originated, but it clearly had been in existence for several years by 1782. It was largely frequented by farmhands and labourers. The low building to the right was a joiner's workshop. These buildings were demolished in 1881 when a more modern version of the public house was opened on an adjoining site.

34. The destruction caused when the Pent Stream rose 6ft. 6ins. in October 1909.

Folkestone Harbour, Fishmarket and Stade

35. This photograph by Venables (1857), now sadly blemished, was probably the first ever taken of the harbour. The sailing ships are probably colliers. Three out of the eight cross-channel paddle-steamer packets are by the quay. A fourth is being repaired on the beach or stade on the left of the photograph. These paddle-steamers were first introduced in 1844 and achieved about 12 knots. In the foreground is the new *Royal Pavilion Hotel*. To the right is the clock tower and harbour offices, which were built in 1843. The branch line to the harbour and the swing bridge were completed in 1849, together with the station.

36. Although the borough council had done much to tidy up the town by 1890, which is roughly when this photograph was taken, and the South-Eastern Railway had caused proper harbour defences to be built, nevertheless the area is still like illustrations seen earlier. To the right of the three cross-channel packets can be seen the workshops, which were not moved to Dover until 1922. Above is the church of St Peter (built in 1862 and enlarged in 1870), in which parish the fishermen lived. To the left is St Peter's School and to the right of the church is St Andrew's convalescent home, which transferred from Guildhall Street in 1884.

37. This view *c*.1896 shows the *London and Paris Hotel* on the extreme left, with part of the *Royal Pavilion Hotel* visible on the right. The Mission to Deep Sea Fishermen's sailing ship is in the immediate foreground. The paddle-steamer is either the *Duchess of York* or the *Princess of Wales*, both of which came into service in 1894.

38. This line, from the old Junction station down to the harbour, has one of the steepest gradients in the country. The train coming down is displaying three white discs on the engine, which usually signifies royalty. The policemen lining the track and the crowd on the quayside underline the probability of it being Queen Victoria's train, Her Majesty en route for the continent, in 1899.

39. In 1904, the new pier promenade was opened to the public. It eased the transfer of passengers between ship and shore.

40. The *Duchess of York* leaving Folkestone c.1898. The departure and arrival of the cross-channel boats were major spectacles for townsfolk and visitors alike.

41. Inner harbour with colliers unloading in about 1908. Such boats, when emptied, often set sail with chalk ballast taken from the Canterbury Road quarry. The *Royal Pavilion Hotel* is on the left, with the *London and Paris Hotel* centre background.

42. One of Smith's carts on its way back to the Tram Road ice store. W. J. Smith established himself as an ice merchant in about 1890 and was one of the first citizens of Folkestone to acquire one of the new-fangled telephones. The ice came from the Scandinavian countries and was used in the fish and hotel trades. As early as July 1855, advertisements appeared in the *Folkestone Chronicle* offering ice for sale at 4s. 0d. a hundredweight.

43.   The South-Eastern and Chatham Railway employed large numbers of 'marine porters' at Folkestone harbour. Each man had his own number clearly displayed on his regulation sweater, so that if there were any problems, he could be easily identified.

44.   These fishing luggers, becalmed just outside Folkestone harbour in about 1880, are seen preparing to row in order to make some headway.

45. (*right*) Dr. William Harvey, the 16th-century son of Folkestone whose work on the circulation of blood won him a place in medical history, together with his brother Sir Eliab Harvey, set up a trust which not only helped to establish a grammar school, but also helped some of the fishermen by buying them boats. The trust abandoned the latter policy in 1858. They had earlier endowed the 'Tanlade' or tan house, seen here *c*.1911. Nets were dipped in 'cutch' to preserve them and on coming out and being dried, they appeared a tan colour. Fishermen paid 8d. to use the Tanlade, which dated from the 17th century. Behind it, note the building with the net loft.

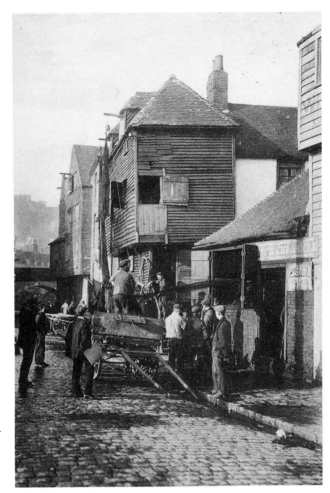

46. (*below*) The fishmarket in action, in about 1906. Tope, locally called 'rig', is being sold in pairs and dog-fish are being auctioned by the score. In between two of the pillars of the fishmarket can be seen a 'pissoir', usually associated with the French, rather than the English, side of the channel. It has long since disappeared.

47. Folkestone's first fishermen's fife and drum band was certainly in existence by 1856. It was disbanded, but reformed towards the end of the century. This photograph, taken in about 1900, shows Sister Katherine keeping a wary eye on the men, who included such characters as 'Bruiser' Marsh with the band mace, Tom Bourne on the bass drum and 'Black'un' William Fagg on the cymbals. Sister Katherine, a nurse, was attached to St Peter's church. She was the driving force behind the band and is said to have allowed them to practise in her cottage, near the end of the stade.

48. Part of the fishmarket in about 1910. The barrows were used to transport fish and shellfish. To the left of the selling shed is the fishermen's Bethel, a chapel and mission hall. Immediately beyond it was the Mission to Deep Sea Fishermen, which was originally a public house called the *North Foreland*. It became, for a time, one of Folkestone Coffee and Refreshment House Company's premises, in which temperance was encouraged. Beyond these two buildings and the railway arch is the *Royal George*.

49. Harvest Festival at the fishermen's Bethel.

50. Taken near what was known as the fishermen's jetty during the early part of this century, this photograph shows fishermen clearing mackerel nets.

51. The Blessing of the Fisheries was first organised in Folkestone by the fishermen's church, St Peter's, probably in June 1890. Seen here in 1927 is Bishop Bidwell, surrounded by his guard of honour of fishermen, together with the incumbent of St Peter's at the time, the Revd. Walter Pickburn. The ceremony usually occurs on the first Sunday after St Peter's Day.

52. Taken in February 1934, this is one of the last photographs of the old fishing quarter before many of the cottages were demolished.

53. The harbour waterfront in 1935. On the left can be seen part of the old fishing village. Demolition work separates that from post-World War One buildings on the right. Above the waterfront stands St Peter's, the fishermen's church, with St Peter's School beyond.

Streets and Trades

54. This old building, known as the Cistern House, stood on the site of the present old town hall. It was built between the years 1782 and 1796. It was a court hall and was a residence for the Earl of Radnor's steward and gaoler. In 1830, the council leased it from Lord Radnor and it was used as a town hall. It was demolished in 1858 to make way for what was to be the new town hall.

55. This photograph dates from just after the opening of the town hall in 1861, the site occupied previously by the Cistern House. The town hall's porch was not added until 1879. The road had been known as Cow Street, but by 1822 it had been changed to the name given to the upper and more modern section of the street—Sandgate Road.

56. This is how Sandgate Road looked in the first years of this century. Adolphus Davis, who dealt in home furnishings, decorating, warehousing and removals, had opened his shop in 1881. On the right is *Bates's Hotel*, a little further down, Lloyd's Bank and on the corner with West Cliff Gardens is the London City and Midland Bank. The town hall can be seen at the bottom of the road.

57. John Sherwood was a grocer, tea dealer and wine and spirit merchant. He began his business in 1852 at the bottom of the old High Street but by 1865 it had moved to No. 1 Sandgate Road. By 1870, it had taken in the site seen here, No. 3 Sandgate Road, where it continued trading until 1921. The founder eventually became an alderman, a J.P. and mayor of Folkestone four times.

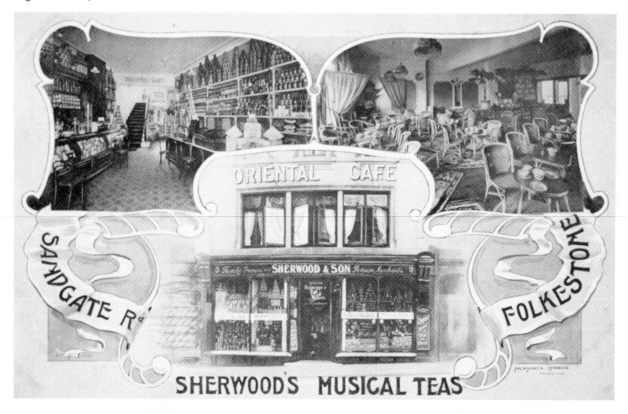

58. (*right*) Carlo Maestrani opened his restaurant in South Street in 1876, calling it the *Cafe Royal*. Nos. 24 & 26 Sandgate Road, as seen here, were built for him in 1889. It was sold in 1932 and pulled down to build the Astoria Cinema, which opened in 1935, later called the Odeon. The site is currently occupied by Boots the chemists.

59. (*below*) Maestrani's high quality restaurant had over 30 staff to run it. Here they are in 1908. In the centre of the front row is Mr. Ronco, who worked at the restaurant for over 50 years, during which time he became its proprietor.

60. Guildhall Street, seen here as it was in the first years of this century, was previously known as Shellons Lane, named after a nearby field. On the left is the *Queen's Hotel*, which was opened in 1885 on the site of the old *King's Arms*. In 1903, it was bought by the Folkestone Hotels Syndicate Ltd., who kept it going, not least through its popular 'Bodega Bar', until 1962.

61. Part of Guildhall Street between 1907 and 1914. On the far left, at No. 19, was J. Franklin, baker and pastrycook. Crossing Queen's Mews, the next dwelling, Ivy House, was occupied by Frank Funnell. He was a job master, fly proprietor and livery stable keeper not only in Queen's Mews, but in Claremont Mews as well. By 1915 he had moved out, probably taking over the *East Kent Arms* in Sandgate Road, so that the site of Ivy House could become the Playhouse and later a supermarket. At No. 23, Marlborough House, lived William Hart, described as a carpenter. H. Hogben, a veterinary surgeon, lived at No. 25, which subsequently became a pharmacy, post office and optician's before the Second World War.

62. Looking down Rendezvous Street in about 1914. Bobby's, on the left, had taken over Clifford Saunders's drapery business by 1907, but in 1925 moved from Rendezvous Street to Sandgate Road and in 1972 were taken over by Debenham's. On the right can be seen Boots, which had also taken over a well-established business, that of John Knight, chemist. Next door, W. C. Stevenson had been trading before the turn of the century, but now called his shop the Army and Navy Cigar Stores. Ainslie Bros., butchers, again next door, had been trading for many years—indeed, Rendezvous Street was originally called Butcher Row. The *Rose Hotel* was first mentioned in 1765 and was one of Folkestone's oldest hostelries, possibly dating from Tudor times. It was a favourite stop for coaches from London, Kent and the Sussex coast. By 1880 it had 16 bedrooms, but it was sold and demolished in 1928.

63. One of the many businesses which came and went relatively quickly was Messrs. Cave, Edwards and Co., whose shop here at No. 3 George Lane, just off Rendezvous Street, was in business from 1908 until 1911.

64. This is how the old High Street looked effectively from the turn of the century to the First World War. This was one of Charles Dickens's favourite streets, down which he strolled during the middle of the last century. It also gives an insight into how much of the town must have looked before Improvement Acts, redevelopment schemes and two World Wars demolished much of old Folkestone.

65. In this photograph, taken in about 1911, Richard Hart, coal merchant, is shown holding his horse. He pursued this trade from 1911 to 1916 from No. 24a Park Road, now called Jesmond Street. This photograph originally belonged to Brian Hart, the local historian.

66. Although this photograph was taken before the First World War, a butcher's shop had been on this Dover Road site for at least 25 years. The shop itself appears to have been built in 1881.

67. The motor transport firm of J. W. Cann. It was based at No. 5 Cheriton Road and Alexandra Mews, Bouverie Road West. It was established in 1902 and later became the London and South Coast Motor Service Ltd. Employees are pictured here outside Portland Place, Dover Road. After several moves, the firm finally closed in 1916.

68. This photograph, taken in 1908, shows the Folkestone winners of the National Union South-Eastern District Westbrook Memorial Challenge Shield, taken at their headquarters at No. 29 Dover Road. By 1915, Folkestone's firefighters consisted of a chief officer, a senior engineer, two engineers, three sub-engineers and 20 firemen. The four horses, which pulled the fire appliances, had to be shared with the Highways Department.

69. (*left*) Dawson's Mill, seen here, was built before 1821. It was situated in Cheriton Road and is commem-orated in the name of Millfield Road. It was offered for sale in 1886 and may well have been demolished and re-erected at Bethersden.

70. Morehall post office *c*.1908. Hughes and Co. opened their business in 1903 and were still there when the First World War broke out. By 1907, they had the post office work too. In the directories of the period they appear as 'Cheriton Avenue' sub-office. L. Keeler, dairyman, had his business next door until 1909.

71. This shop, displaying its Christmas wares at No. 14 Bouverie Road West, was, from 1896 to 1906, the West End and Poultry Stores. From 1907-24, it was John Bailey, fishmonger and poulterer, while from 1925-36, as Macfisheries Ltd., it continued as a fishmonger and poulterer. Mr. Palmer, the man in the white apron, was manager, although the date of this photograph is uncertain.

72. The *King's Arms Hotel*, seen here in about 1875, stood on this site from 1796 and possibly earlier. It was later to be demolished in 1881, in order to make way for the *Queen's Hotel*. The Medhurst family ran the hotel for at least two generations.

73. (*left*) Typical of the small hotels in Folkestone was the *Belle-Vue* in St John's Street. Opened in about 1855, it was noted as a good place to purchase fish. The *Belle-Vue* was owned for many years by the grandfather of Alan Taylor who has contributed many of the pictures reproduced in this book. The hotel finally closed in 1925.

74. (*below*) This rather odd picture of the *Bouverie Arms* seems to date from its opening, which was *c*.1859. Although it still thrives, its backdrop today, from the same angle, is a multi-storey car park.

75. The *Royal Pavilion Hotel* was built initially by the South-Eastern Railway. In 1889, no longer in railway hands, it was virtually rebuilt to accommodate 230 guests. The hotel attracted royalty and the cream of society. The photograph shows it at the beginning of this century, when its popularity and influence were just starting to wane. It kept going until the middle of this century. *Motel Burstin*, which partly stands on its site today, has taken part of its trade, but it has not been able to recapture the *Royal Pavilion*'s sheer grandeur.

76. Although originally four houses, known as Langhorne Gardens, these properties were bought up by a Mr. Masters in 1857 and were opened as the *West Cliff Hotel* in August of that year under G. Giovanni, former manager of the *Royal Pavilion Hotel*. A new wing was added in 1860 and the hotel's magnificent ballroom was much admired. During the First World War, the *West Cliff* was used for troops. It was renamed the *Majestic* and survived until 1962, when it was demolished. This view of 1904 shows it at the height of its popularity.

The Leas

77. This comparatively rare photograph, taken in the early 1880s, gives a superb panoramic view of the Leas, Lower Sandgate Road, the Marine Gardens and the harbour, where a few masted ships, as well as a cross-channel packet, can be seen. Bathing carriages, too, are much in evidence.

78. A view of the Leas from its west end, during the first years of this century. Part of it was still being used as a meadow. The old Metropole Bandstand is shown, while to the left of it is the *Metropole* itself. Further on is the *Grand Hotel*, while beyond the *Grand* can be seen the Manor House.

79. The Metropole Lift was opened on 31 March 1904, some time after the appearance of the Leas Lifts and the Sandgate Lift. It was installed specifically for those staying in the *Metropole* and the *Grand* to allow them to get to Lower Sandgate Road easily. It had the shortest track of the four lifts, being only 96ft. long. It was boarded up during the Second World War and never used again.

80. Taken just after the First World War, this view shows the upper Leas on the right, with Madeira Walk, a little sunken, to the left. Originally the latter was known as 'Cow Path', as cows had beaten their own track in order to reach the more inviting grass just below the top of the cliff. Further along Madeira Walk can be seen the Metropole Lift and, nearby, the Metropole or West Leas Bandstand, which was originally built behind the *Metropole* and was transferred to the site seen here in 1902. Since then it has been demolished. To the right is the *Grand Hotel*, built in 1904 and opened in 1905. Its white painted conservatory became known as the 'Monkey House', as people would often come and stare at the people sitting inside, in the hope of seeing someone famous. Beyond the *Grand* is the *Metropole*, which was completed in 1897.

81. (*left*) This statue of William Harvey (1578-1657), Folkestone's most famous son, was by Albert Joy and was unveiled in 1881. Every year on 1 April, the great man's birthday, there is a wreath-laying ceremony attended by representatives of the medical profession. This photograph was taken *c*.1905.

82. (*below*) This view of the Leas shows the old Leas Shelter in the foreground, erected by the Earl of Radnor and leased to the Borough Corporation to be run by the Folkestone Amusement Association in 1894. It contained a 62ft. by 31ft. central hall. An orchestra played daily in spring, autumn and winter, while a band played in the summer when it was wet. The shelter is seen here with its old roof *c*.1905. Part of the Victoria Pier can be seen in the distance and the bandstand in Marine Gardens is also visible.

83. The Leas Cliff Hall just before its opening in 1927 by Prince Henry. It replaced the Leas Shelter built in 1894 and it cost £80,000 (*see* plates 171 and 172).

85. Another unusual sight on the Leas in the 1930s was this llama and trap among the bathchairs.

84. This shows one of the more original modes of transport available on the Leas in 1895. Note the carefully-groomed ladies in the background, some complete with their parasols, taking the air.

86. The Leas Bandstand at dusk, taken in about 1915. This bandstand was erected in 1895, although bands playing on the promenade had been organised since 1867. Note the lamplighters at work and the bathchairs and their attendants still pushing and pulling their clients along.

87. Early in 1885, the Folkestone Lift Company was formed. On 16 September the same year, Regatta Day, the first lift was opened at a cost of about £3,000 to the company. The track was 164ft. long. Such was the demand that in August 1890 a second lift was opened— the one nearer to the camera in this 1902 photograph. It had to be built a little closer to the vertical and as a consequence the track was shorter than that of the other lift—a mere 155ft. long. They both survived the two World Wars but in the 1960s it was decided that the 1890 lift was not required. It took its last passengers on 27 October 1966. The other lift was taken over by the council in the summer of 1967, when the lift company went into voluntary liquidation.

88. This shows the original front of the Leas Pavilion when it opened as tea rooms. Reginald Pope, the architect, was aware that the hotels either side enjoyed long leases from the Earl of Radnor, which included the 'ancient lights' clause stating that there could be no restriction on the daylight through hotel windows. The solution was to build below ground level. On 1 July 1902 Lord Radnor opened the £10,000 building.

89. The Leas Pavilion Tea Rooms were the idea of Mr. Frederick Ralph. When they were opened, provision was made for musical accompaniment from the balcony. A ladies' string trio provided a novel attraction, with a vocalist joining in from time to time. Luncheons were 2s. 6d., while afternoon tea was 6d. These expensive prices were so that only the highest class of visitor would patronise the tea rooms. In 1928 'Jimmy' Grant Anderson built a stage and introduced the tea matinee. In 1929 Mr. Anderson left and the Arthur Brough Players moved in.

90. This 1910 view from the east end of the Leas overlooking the completed harbour shows in the foreground the Weston memorial, named after Sydney Cooper Weston (1842-93), photographer, philanthropist and temperance advocate. It was unveiled in February 1898. The memorial was later removed to East Cliff, where it still stands. The hansom cabs could be hired for up to 2s. 6d. per hour, while the bathchairs would have cost one shilling per hour. The prices had moved little since the 1860s.

91. This photograph, probably taken just before the First World War, shows the Tudor gun which was said to date from 1550 and to have come from the battery on the Bayle. It stood upended outside the *Shakespeare*, at the junction of Guildhall Street and Cheriton Road, before being mounted on a carriage and moved to this site in about 1911. It remained on the Leas until the early 1920s, when it was moved to the corporation pound off Warren Road. Later, it was sold for scrap. To the left is the Weston Memorial and the cab and bathchair ranks. Beyond are Albion Villas, which had only just been built when Charles Dickens rented No. 3 in 1855 for three months, while he was working on his book *Little Dorrit*. Beyond is the tower of the parish church.

92.   The man in uniform was Albert Burvill who was a policeman for the Earl of Radnor. It was his job to keep trespassers out of the private parks in the middle of such desirable squares as Grimston Gardens. It was also his task to try to keep undesirables off the Leas, as it was felt that only ladies and gentlemen and people of quality should be allowed to mingle there.

The Beach Along
Lower Sandgate Road

93. This very early photograph of *c*.1860 shows Folkestone Gas Works, which were opened in December 1842, standing on part of what later became the Marine Crescent site. When it first opened, it served 60 private consumers and 30 street lamps. Demand increased so much that these gas works were demolished in 1866, when a new works opened in Foord Road. In the background, the building with the clock tower housed the harbour offices. A train can be seen crossing the swing bridge.

94.   Building began on the Bathing Establishment in 1867. The company's publicity said that the object was: 'To supply the town of Folkestone, and the numerous visitors who resort thereunto, for the sake of its salubrious and invigorating air, with Hot, Cold, Vapour, Shower, Swimming, Medicated and other Baths'. It went on to state that: 'The Baths, Swimming Bath and Hot Water Apparatus are on the ground floor. The upper portion is devoted to Reception and Recreation Rooms, Reading and Billiard Rooms, and a large Saloon, immediately over the Swimming Bath (with Balconies facing the Sea) for the meeting of Subscribers and Entertainments'. It was completed in time for the 1869 season. It was thought very fashionable and rather like a London club, but with some interesting additions. It did not finally close until 1958.

95.   In the 1880s a local man, Mr. W. D. Fagg, invented the carriages shown on the rails in the photograph. They had two advantages over the ordinary bathing carriage. Firstly, they overcame the shelving problem of the beach. Secondly, they provided improved security for the clothing and valuables of wealthy visitors.

FOLKESTONE
BATHING ESTABLISHMENT CO., LTD.

Private Baths (Hot and Cold) in Sea or Fresh Water.
From 7 a.m. to 7.30 p.m. Sundays (during
the Season), from 7 to 9.30 a.m.

LADIES' AND GENTLEMEN'S SEA WATER SWIMMING BATHS.

Hot & Cold Sea Water delivered in the Town.

REFRESHMENT AND BILLIARD-ROOMS.

SEA BATHING FROM THE FORESHORE.

FAGG'S NEW & IMPROVED SAFETY BATHING CARRIAGE (Patent No. 3217).

FAGG'S PATENT BATHING CARRIAGE comprises a number of cabins on an iron frame fitted with wheels, running on a tram line. The floor is horizontal, and remains so at all states of the tide. The carriage is drawn up and let down by a wire rope, and can be worked by hand, gas, or other power. The cabins open on either side into a corridor. At the sea end is a safety crate, in which non-swimmers can bathe in safety. Diving boards are arranged at the sides and end of the crate, from which a "header" can be taken into deep water, a thing unsafe from an ordinary machine.

An attendant is in waiting to supply towels, etc. He also has charge of the key of the cabin, thus security is insured of the property of bathers.

The carriage can be entered from the shore end at any time, and the bather can leave after taking his bath, without inconvenience of loss of time.

The carriage travels smoothly on the rails, and it is easily adjusted to the rise and fall of the tide.

The Patentee will be happy to give further particulars as to cost of construction, working, and Patent rights, on application.

W. D. FAGG,
Bathing Establishment, Folkestone.

Mr. F. E. BECKWITH, *Professor of Swimming, Royal Aquarium, S.W.; Teacher to the Head Educational Institutions of England; and promoter of the useful art for forty years.*

Mr. W. D. FAGG, Dec. 23rd, 1889.—My dear Sir,—The many seaside places I and family visit round the United Kingdom, teaching and giving Swimming Entertainments, makes me thoroughly understand the want of such a Bathing Carriage as you have, after a deal of patience and skill, invented. I beg to add my opinion of its great merit, and congratulate you on the same.
Yours truly, F. E. BECKWITH.

96. Advertisement from 1896/7 Pike's Directory for the Folkestone Bathing Establishment.

97.　The foundation stone for the Victoria Pier was laid by Viscountess Folkestone on 7 May 1887. She also opened the completed pier on 21 July 1888. It was nearly 700ft. long and 30ft. wide. The pavilion at the end seated about 1,000. Music hall stars such as Marie Lloyd appeared there. In 1910, a skating rink was added on the west side of the entrance. The ornamental garden on the east side was illuminated at night and concerts were sometimes given there. The pavilion was destroyed by fire on Whit Monday, 1945. The pier, which had originally cost £44,000, was finally dismantled in 1954.

98.　The first lifeboat, the *J. McConnel Hussey*, arrived in November 1893, when the station was established. The cost of the boat carriage and equipment was met by a Miss Curling of Denmark Hill, London. The best-known lifeboat on the Folkestone station was probably the self-righting *Leslie*, which served from 1904-30. The station closed down in October 1930.

99. A lease for a switchback railway was granted in 1891. The American invention proved extremely popular. A Mr. Sinclair, 'Uncle Tom', of Pavilion Road was the owner for many years and records that Mrs. Asquith was so entranced with it that she persuaded her husband, the Prime Minister, to have a go. The Princesses Helene, Louise and Isabella of Orleans often went on it. Sir Edward Sassoon's family, the Rothschilds, General Sir Baker Russell and the Bishop of Birmingham were all very staid figures who thoroughly enjoyed the switchback.

100. This unusual angle, taken c.1910, gives a very good victim's eye view of the switchback track.

101. Pleasure-boat men in the 1930s on the shingle close to Marine Parade and the Marine Gardens Bandstand waiting for the wind to drop, so that they could take visitors out in their rowing boats. It cost 3s. 0d. to hire them for an hour. If you just hired the boat, it cost 2s. 3d.

102. Folkestone Regatta Day seen from the end of Folkestone Pier at about the turn of the century.

Other Places of Recreation

103. This rather faded view shows Radnor Park 10 years or so after it was opened by Viscount Folkestone, M.P., on 9 June 1886. It was presented to the borough by Viscount Folkestone's father, the Earl of Radnor. The original size was some 20 acres, but it was later added to, on the north side. There were lawns and flower-beds, as well as boating ponds at one end. In the photograph, the Royal Victoria Hospital can be seen in the background on the right. The house in the foreground is the park keeper's lodge, while the shelter in front of it was for the cab drivers.

104. The Bayle Pond is reputed to be the site where St Eanswythe allowed the water, which she had brought by aqueduct from a spring near the foot of the North Downs, to flow out. This photograph, taken at about the turn of the century, shows the pond as it was rather than the small ornamental affair it is today.

Folkestone Rover.
F. Funnell, Proprietor.

Queen's Mews, Folkestone.

105. During the first years of this century, many were reluctant to see the age of the horse give way to that of the motor car and charabanc. Several cashed in on this feeling. In Folkestone, Frank Funnell ran a four-horse coach service to Canterbury. In 1914 the fare was 10s. return, plus 2s. 6d. each way if you wanted a converted box seat next to the coachman. The service was only offered in the height of summer, from July to September.

106.   The 'Active' coach time-table.

The "ACTIVE" Coach Time Table.

Outward Journey.

	a.m.
EAST KENT ARMS HOTEL, Folkestone	10.45
METROPOLE Hotel, Folkestone	11 0
QUEEN'S Hotel, Folkestone	11.10
HAWKINGE	11.40
SWINGFIELD	11.45
SELSTED...	11.55
DENTON	p.m. 12.5
BRIDGE	1.0
COUNTY HOTEL, CANTERBURY ...	1.20

Homeward Journey.

	p.m.
Leaving Canterbury ...	4.0
Bridge	4.20
DENTON	5.5
Leaving Denton	5.25
Arriving Folkestone ...	6.30

BOXING NIGHT,
December 26th, 1887.

TOWN HALL,
FOLKESTONE.

MR. TOM TAYLOR begs to announce to his numerous Friends
that he will give a

VARIETY

Entertainment

Assisted by the following :

THE SISTERS ALBANY
(ANNIE AND ETTY),

The X L C R Vocalists and Premier Lady Duettists and Dancers·

MR. W. GLANFIELD
The Popular Bass.

BROTHERS HUNT
Negro Sketch Artists.

Master Loftus Wilfred Taylor
(Better known as Chip Taylor),
Character Comic Singer and Dancer.

THE RIDGWAY TRIO
Albert, Marie and Little Bert.
In their unrivalled Musical Sketch.

Tom Taylor
Character Comic Singer.

Doors open at 7.15   The Band will play in the Hall from 7.30 to 8.

Admission : Front Seats, 2s.   Second, 1s.   Gallery, 6d.

J. English, Printer & Lithograper, Folkestone & Hythe.

107.   The town hall was one of the key places of entertainment during the latter part of
Queen Victoria's reign. Here is a handbill for Boxing Night, 1887.

108. This humorous card dates from the first few years of this century and was a form of advertising favoured by Charles Major, when he was landlord of the *East Kent Arms*.

109. In 1886 the Folkestone Art Treasures Exhibition Company was formed. It erected a hall rather like the Crystal Palace to house the various *objets d'art* which had been assembled. Electricity—possibly the first used in Folkestone—was installed. A special railway line from Shorncliffe station, now Folkestone West, was laid, but closed after five months. The building was sold and soon became the Pleasure Gardens Theatre, which seated 1,500 people. In 1913 the foyer was enlarged into a spacious concert hall. Just off the theatre was a gymnasium and the complex was surrounded by 16 acres of gardens in which lawn tennis, croquet and skating could be enjoyed, as well as military bands and orchestras. The complex finally closed in 1960.

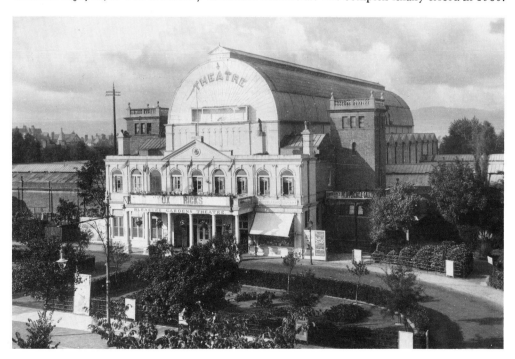

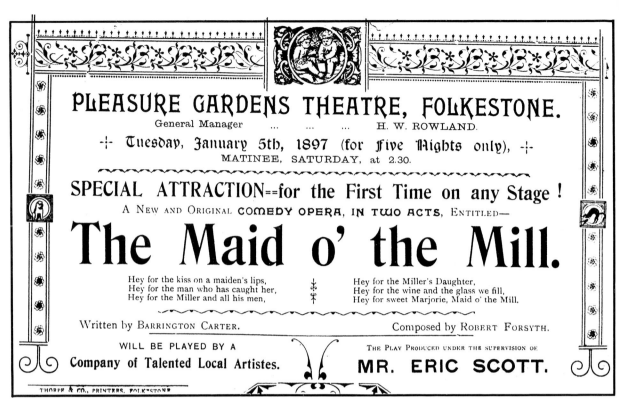

110. Publicity, January 1897-style, for 'The Maid O'The Mill'. This was one of the earlier productions put on when the original exhibition area had been turned into a theatre.

111. Prices for theatre admission.

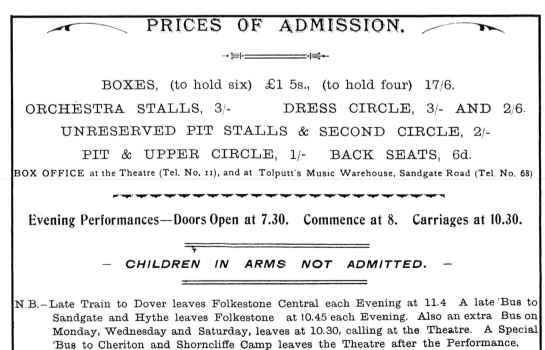

112.   This gives a view of the Pleasure Gardens in about 1915. From the croquet lawn can be seen a large audience attending a band concert. Beyond is the theatre itself.

113.   This 1925 view of the Pleasure Gardens from the air shows the extent of the grounds in Bouverie Road West.

114. This rare view shows the interior of the Art Treasures Exhibition in 1886, with exhibits on display. Note the stained glass at the back, together with the three-manual organ.

115. One of the more popular attractions to the Pleasure Gardens were military tournaments, this one in 1905.

116. This was taken in about 1915, soon after the Central Picture Theatre opened in George Lane. It could seat approximately 800 at either 3d., 6d. or one shilling per seat. It is the only Folkestone cinema to have survived until today. It is now the Classic cinema, though divided into three studios.

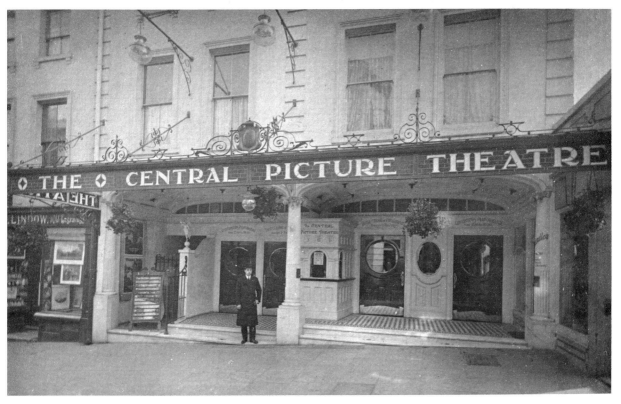

117. The Electric Theatre, Folkestone Picture Playhouse, arrived in Folkestone either late in 1910 or early in 1911 at No. 1 Grace Hill. It replaced a garage. A February 1911 programme shows that between 3 p.m. and 10.30 p.m. on any day the continuous programme showed eight different films. The invitation, issued so soon after the cinema's opening, was a masterly public relations idea, possibly thought up by the company's secretary, William White. The coronation film was shown a mere eight days after the event itself. The cinema survived a fire in 1928 and two World Wars, although it became the *Savoy* en route. It was an eventual casualty to television.

118. Before the Leas Cliff Hall and the Pleasure Gardens Theatre came into being, the town hall in Sandgate Road was often used for lectures and concerts (*see* plate 55). Here is an end-of-season playbill of 1893.

Churches and Chapels

119. This statue of St Eanswythe, patron saint of
Folkestone and of the parish church, as well as founder
and first abbess of a community at Folkestone, is to be
found in the south chapel of the parish church. It was
restored in 1927. St Eanswythe was a Kentish princess
and tradition suggests that she arrived in Folkestone
about A.D. 630. St Eanswythe's Day is 12 September.

St. Eanswythe was the daughter of Eadbald.
She founded the First Sisterhood in England,
on the banks of the cliffs near Folkestone in A.D. 630

120. This copy of a painting c.1850 shows the poor
level of maintenance inside the parish church which
greeted Matthew Woodward when he became vicar in
1851. Over the next four decades, the church was to
be transformed into the beautiful building it is today.

121.　This shows the exterior state of the parish church *c*.1850. The graveyard was overfull.
The makeshift west end, with its three odd-looking windows and peculiar roof, had been built
as a temporary measure as a result of the great storm of 1705, which had destroyed two bays at
the west end of the church. At the time, it was thought pointless to do much as it would not be
long before the cliff, with the church, would fall into the sea. This was not to be.

122.　This very rare photograph of 1864, looking down Westcliff Gardens, shows the parish church
with its new west end, but before the Harvey window was installed.

123.   This 1885 view of the parish church shows it much as it is known today. During Canon Woodward's incumbency, the church west of the tower had been taken down, extended by 40ft. and widened. The Harvey west window was completed in 1874 and paid for by the British medical profession, as a memorial to Dr. William Harvey.

124. Christ Church, Sandgate Road, was originally built to serve the westward-growing town in 1850. This was how the interior looked in 1905. The entire building, except for the clocktower, was destroyed by a German bomb on 17 May 1942.

125. This shows Christ Church in about 1870. Originally built in 1850 on land donated by the Earl of Radnor, it gradually expanded, finally having a clocktower. After the church was bombed in May 1942, the area was created, and still remains, a small park.

126. In 1864 Mr. John Harvey gave some land so that a mission church could be built in the Dover Road area. On 12 July 1865 a wooden church, seating 600, was opened. It quickly became known as the 'Red Barn'. The foundation stone for a more substantial building was laid by the Revd. Matthew Woodward on 17 April 1873. St Michael's was consecrated on 3 August 1875, a further aisle being completed in 1884. F. Bodley was the church's architect. It was finally demolished in 1954.

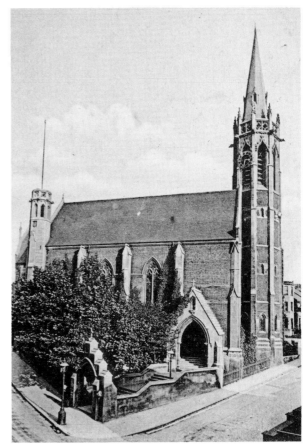

127. This shows the interior of St Michael's in about 1904. Seated at the four-manual Henry Jones organ is the Revd. Edward Husband (1843-1908), who was vicar, organist and choirmaster from 1873 until his death. He was an innovator, introducing popular events such as the Cyclists' Service, which was noted in the national press. He was also chaplain to 'D' (Folkestone) Company of the Buffs, an inventor of musical effects, composer, traveller, lecturer and strong supporter of local charities.

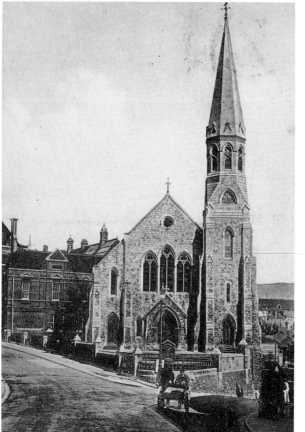

128. In 1797 the Congregationalists broke away from the Folkestone Anabaptists, from whom they had developed. In 1856 they built this church at the top of Tontine Street, which they later enlarged. Originally it had a spire, but it was removed as its weight was causing subsidence due to the Pent Stream passing several feet beneath the foundations. Their church by Radnor Park was not opened until 1897. This Tontine Street church was eventually taken down in 1974.

129. Folkestone Wesleyan Methodists formed a group in 1824, meeting in a room in Elgar's Yard. They had a small chapel in the old High Street in 1831 and built another in Sandgate Road next to the *King's Arms* in 1852. It was decided that Folkestone would be the headquarters of a circuit and so in 1864 they began to build this church, where Grace Hill meets the Dover Road. It was opened on 31 March 1866 and was finally demolished in 1976. The library behind it, opened in 1888 by the local M. P., Sir Edward Watkin, was originally on the Bayle from 1879. Andrew Carnegie, the Scots millionaire philanthropist, in large measure paid for a wing to be added in 1910.

East Cliff and The Warren

130. The old *Warren Inn* at East Cliff, pictured in about 1880. Its licence was finally withdrawn in 1892. Behind it can be seen a Martello Tower.

131. This shows Copt Point, East Cliff *c.*1910. The chimneys and roofs behind the hedges belonged to the old *Warren Inn*, now turned into tea-rooms. The building had gone by 1924. The Martello Tower in the background is no. 3.

ZIGZAG PATH. WARREN. FOLKESTONE.

132.   Warren Halt in about 1914. The train stopped for visitors who wished to wander around the Warren and, via the zig-zag path, the cliffs. The tea-room and the halt survived the Second World War, but not for long.

133.   Loading hay on East Cliff in the 1920s. In the background, the harbour can be dimly seen. The track running uphill is roughly where Wear Bay is today.

134. In 1924 exciting discoveries were made on East Cliff. Villas of two periods of Roman life were uncovered. They remained on show to the public until 1954 when, partly because of bomb damage, they were covered over again by the borough council. It is thought by some that the earlier villa may have been built before A.D. 100. A further villa was built at right angles to the first. They were inhabited until about A.D. 350. This photograph shows the Roman site looking south.

135. The Roman site, showing the main corridor and rooms adjoining.

136. This 1920s view across the whole East Cliff area shows how little there was, apart from the Martello Towers and Warren Farm in the foreground, now long since gone.

137. The East Cliff between the wars, at about the time when the Earl of Radnor gave a large part of this area to the town. As yet, there is no East Cliff Pavilion, which was built roughly where the vertically-striped hut is in the photograph, in 1934.

Other Glimpses of Bygone Folkestone

138. The funeral of some of the victims of the crew of the *Grosser Kurfurst*, who drowned when their warship collided with another German vessel or Ironclad off Sandgate on 31 May 1878. The service was held in the Cheriton Road cemetery, where there is still a monument, erected by the German government in 1881, to the 287 men who were lost.

139. This drinking fountain was erected in February 1860 in Kingsbridge Street (now Harbour Street). W. Tiffen was in business in the street as bookseller, printer and stationer from 1847-74. Tiffen's were well known for their local guides which not only covered Folkestone, but also Hythe and the surrounding countryside.

140. The Royal Victoria was originally a charitable hospital, which resulted from a dispensary founded by Dr. Donnelly in 1845. Demand for medical help increased so much that Queen Victoria's Jubilee provided a suitable reason for the Earl of Radnor to give an acre or so of ground for a new hospital in 1887. It was built in 1889 and was opened by Alfred, Duke of Edinburgh, on 3 July 1890. This photograph was taken just after the turn of the century.

141.   Sgt. Albert Ames (centre) of No. 29 Charlotte Street, Folkestone, with some privates outside the drill hall, Shellons Street. 'D' Company of the fourth battalion of the county regiment, the 'Buffs', were traditionally recruited from the Folkestone area.

CERTIFICATE OF SERVICE

This is to Certify~

that *Sergt Albert Ross Ames*

served in *1st Vol. Battn The Buffs (E. Kent Regt)* fro

the *Twentyseventh* day of *January* 18

till the *Thirtyfirst* day of *March* 19

having served continuously for

Twenty years *Sixtyfour* days

Corps in which service was given

1st Vol Battn The Buffs (East Kent Regt)

Campaigns and Medals

Volunteer long service medal

Police Ambulance medal Coronation 1902

Asaqel LT-GENL,

COMMANDING-IN-CHIEF, EASTERN COMMAND.

Dieu et mon droit

142. Long-service certificate awarded to Sgt. Albert Ames.

143. One of the few photographs showing
the mayor and corporation outside the town
hall. It was taken during the summer of 1909
when the mayor, Albert Pepper, accompanied by A. F. Kidson, the town clerk and
Edwin Chadwick, the town sergeant,
received troops from Shorncliffe Camp when
they marched through the town.

144. The founder of the modern Sassoon
dynasty was David Sassoon, who was born in
1792 of Jewish parents in Baghdad. Via
Persia and later India, the family finally settled in London. In 1899 Sir Edward Sassoon
was elected M.P. for Hythe, which included
Folkestone, with a majority of 527 for the
Conservatives. He remained M.P. until his
death on 12 May 1912. In the resulting by-
election, his son, Sir Philip Sassoon, was
elected. Sir Philip was later private secretary to General Haig and to Prime Minister
Lloyd George.

YOUR OLD AND TRIED MEMBER
EDWARD A. SASSOON

TOO GOOD
TO LOSE

145. The Holy Trinity cricket team of 1913. The priest holding the cup, Canon Frederic Gardiner, was vicar. What makes the picture of particular interest is that it was taken in a field which no longer exists, between Salters laundry and what is now Alder Road.

146. Polling day, 22 January 1910, in Folkestone. For the fourth time Sir Edward Sassoon was to be returned, this time with a Conservative majority of 1,792 over the Liberal, W. Clarke Hall.

147. The proclamation of King George V being read out at the town hall on 11 May 1910.

The First World War

148.   One of the best-known faces in Folkestone had to leave very quickly on
the outbreak of war in August 1914. Moritz Worms, a native of Lemborg, Prussia,
which is now a part of Poland, was renowned for his violin playing. His Blue
Viennese Band was one of the most popular in town.

149.   The First World War started for Britain on 4 August 1914. These German nationals had been rounded up by 10 August and were being marched off as prisoners to Shorncliffe Camp.

150.   A few days after the German nationals had been sent to Shorncliffe Camp, the Austrian nationals were arrested on 13 August. They are seen here being marched from Sandgate High Street into Military Road.

151. At least two squadrons of cavalry on parade at Shorncliffe Camp, a few months before the outbreak of the First World War.

152. Belgian soldiers, possibly medical orderlies, having just come ashore in the first weeks of the war. Behind them are refugees. About 65,000 Belgians were cared for by Folkestone townspeople and the Belgian Committee for Refugees in the first few months of the war.

153.   Some of the craft which brought the refugees across the English Channel from Belgium in 1914.

154.   These soldiers from the Belgian Cycle Corps had to evacuate from Dieppe to Folkestone. They had fought the Germans at Namur but had become detached from their main unit. Within 24 hours of arriving they had made arrangements to go back to continue fighting. This photograph shows them on the Folkestone Pier just before their departure.

155. J. Anderson, town crier during the First World War and for many years afterwards, composed fiercely patriotic verse which was published in this postcard form.

156. Sir Stephen Penfold (1842-1925) emerging after a service at the parish church in 1915. A Folkestone wine merchant by occupation, he was knighted on 1 January 1915. He was first mayor six times between 1888 and 1912, and then continuously from 1913 to 1919. Carrying the mace on this occasion was the town sergeant, Edwin Chadwick, and the mayor is being accompanied by the chief constable of Folkestone, Mr. Harry Reeve, who commanded a force which at that time consisted of himself, three inspectors, four sergeants, a detective-sergeant and 38 constables. The town clerk, Mr. A. F. Kidson, can also be seen.

A Call to Arms.

Lord Kitchener's appeal has been nobly responded to,
But still your King and Country need you.
Young men, rally round the flag that for ever will fly,
For Britishers know how to fight and to die.
And England's brave daughters are not behind.
They've left their homes, gone to the front to nurse the sick
                                  their wounds to bind.
Inspired with love, they're true Miss Nightingales.
God bless our daughters and the Prince of Wales.

A Dream of War.

I dreamt a dream, an awful dream, I dreamt of War.

I saw our enemies invading the English shore.

The sight was awful to behold.

The slaughter of children, women, young and old.

Midst fire and blood and cannon smoke.

From such a scene, I awoke

Methought such things can never be

When British ships are on the sea,

Manned by Bluejackets, staunch and true

And our brave British Soldiers on land fight for me and you

Sons of Peasants, Dukes and Peers,

Face the enemy ; they have no fears.

Shoulder to shoulder, hand to hand

These gallant lads fight on sea and land.

Proud waves the Royal Standard and the Union Jack,

The enemy will never see an Englishman's back.

For King and Country is our battle cry,

On to Victory or we die.

Victory is ours, loud let it ring

With a mighty shout—

GOD SAVE THE KING.

Composed by

J. Anderson, Town Crier. Folkestone.

COPYRIGHT.

157.   This well-known photograph of King George V, accompanied by Lord Kitchener, shows him riding through Cheriton, having just passed the *White Lion Hotel*, in September 1915. He had been inspecting the Canadian troops at Shorncliffe Camp. This photograph was taken by H. B. Green, photographer and picture frame maker, only a few feet away from his business premises in Risborough Lane. (His nephew, Roy, kindly made the print available.)

158.   A potato queue in Cheriton High Street in 1916.

BOROUGH OF FOLKESTONE.

FOLKESTONE BOROUGH EDUCATION COMMITTEE.

THE GREAT WAR
The National Cause and Self-sacrifice.

Public Elementary Schools Breaking upday.
Summer Holiday 1917.

In order that the Scholars may have a part in the Great War in which the Country is engaged, Diplomas are presented a **third** *year instead of Books.*

This is to Certify *that* Elsie Marsh
has gained the

Prize for *History & Composition*
in Class IV *of the* Girls'
Department *of the* Dover Rd. Council *School.*

E. A. Welch.
Head Teacher.

Stephen Penfold
Mayor of Folkestone and
Chairman of the Education Committee.

Thos Wilkinson
Clerk of the Committee

G. Morgan
Alderman, Vice Chairman
of the Education Committee.

159.   This school certificate, given to Elsie Marsh in 1917, was instead of a book, which was the customary prize, so that money saved thereby could be donated to the war effort. The certificate is of interest as it shows the signature of Sir Stephen Penfold, who had been knighted in 1915 and had an unrivalled record as the man who had been mayor of Folkestone most often.

160. Another way of making money was to send round 'Gebby', who collected a considerable amount for the Belgian refugees.

Thinking of you day by day.

A Greeting from Folkestone.

161. The strains of separation are clearly expressed in this card of the First World War. Folkestone was a huge transit camp, being the main embarkation point for the continent through which tens of thousands of men passed on their way to the battlefields of France and Belgium. It was also a main reception area for the wounded.

162.   The Manor House on the Leas, belonging to the Earl of Radnor, was, like many other large houses and hotels in Folkestone, used as a hospital for wounded soldiers during the First World War. Although it contained 15 bed- and dressing rooms, three bathrooms, four large reception rooms and quarters for domestic staff, its accommodation had to be supplemented—hence the marquees on the lawn in this photograph of 1917.

163.   The Folkestone Big Gun Week, from 14 to 20 July 1918, was a campaign to raise money for war loans. This photograph, which was taken on the Leas opposite Albion Villas, shows among others, Sir Stephen Penfold, mayor of Folkestone during the war, sixth from the left. Third from the left is Mr. R. Forsyth, who was managing director of Folkestone's Victoria Pier.

Army Form B. 55.

Great Britain and Ireland.

Applicable only during the emergency commencing on 4th August, 1914.

To the OCCUPIER (name) _____*Mrs Willer*_____
(See Note A).

at _*66 Morehall Avenue.*_ Street, in the Parish of _____*Folkestone*_____

    In accordance with the provisions of the Army Act you are hereby required to find Quarters for—

OFFICERS AND MEN—

    Class I.   .... Lodging and Attendance for_____officers_____men

    Class II.   .... Lodging and Attendance for____*4*____men

    Class III.   .... Unfurnished Accommodation for_____officers_____men

    The Military Authorities are empowered to call upon you to provide meals as well as quarters for soldiers.

HORSES—

    Class I.   .... Proper Stabling with forage for _____horses

    Class II.   .... Proper Stabling without forage for _____horses

    Class III.   .... Covered Accommodation only for_____horses

of the _*Royal Engineers*_ Regiment, from _*24th Oct*_to_____(if period known).

Dated the_____*24th*_____day of_____*October*_____19*17*.

_____*Billet Master.*

Overleaf are shown :—

    The accommodation to be provided under each class.

    The quantities of food and drink to be supplied to soldiers (if you are required to supply meals) as fixed by His Majesty's Regulations.

    The rates of payment for accommodation, meals, etc.

NOTE A.—In time of national emergency the occupiers of all public buildings, dwelling-houses, warehouses, barns, and stables are, as well as the keepers of victualling houses, liable to provide billets, with or without meals.

(6203)   W 12223/R1020   500,000   12/16   McA. & W., Ltd.   (E. 741)   **[P.T.O.**

164. This billet form for soldiers was handed to Mrs. Willer of No. 66 Morehall Avenue in 1917. She was required to provide lodging '. . . with bed and attendance', but no meals for four Royal Engineers. For this she was paid 6d. per man per day. Among the notes, it is pointed out that the officers had to pay for their own food and that as far as horses were concerned, 'The manure remains the property of the War Department which is entitled to keep any benefit arising from its disposal'.

165. There were at least four rest camps situated in various parts of Folkestone during the First World War. This rest camp was situated mainly on Marine Parade, which was virtually the closest point to disembarkation possible for troops coming back from the continent.

Between the Wars and Floral Folkestone

166. This German U-boat arrived in Folkestone harbour on 3 January 1919.
U64 was open to the public to inspect.

167. This peace tea, held on the bank holiday of 4 August 1919, was organised by Mrs. A. G. Gales and Mrs. A. V. Minter for over 100 children from Radnor Street and North Street. Skipper T. Nicks of the fishermen's Bethel presided. Each child went away with a gift of a threepenny bit.

168. On 29 July 1919 this World War One tank was presented to the town by Sir E. Swinton, who had played a key role in its invention. It was kept on the Durlocks. It is said that it was used for scrap for World War Two.

169.   This War Memorial on the Leas was erected and dedicated in 1922.

170.   A young Prince of Wales, afterwards Edward VIII, laying the foundation stone of the nurses' quarters at the Royal Victoria Hospital, Folkestone, on 27 July 1921.

171. This unique photograph, sadly marred by light, shows the opening of the Leas Cliff Hall on Wednesday 13 July 1927 by Prince Henry of Teck. To the right of the Prince, who stands in the middle of the photograph in army uniform, stands the mayor, Alderman Reginald Wood. To the left of Prince Henry can be seen a B.B.C. microphone, as his speech and that of the mayor was broadcast throughout the British Isles. The Prince was presented with a gold key by the architect, J. L. Seaton Dahl. The Leas Cliff Hall (see plate 83) replaced the old Leas Shelter.

WOOD · MAYOR.

BOROUGH OF FOLKESTONE.

VISIT OF

H.R.H. The Prince Henry

WEDNESDAY, JULY 13th, 1927.

Official Programme.

172. Official programme for Prince Henry's visit, 1927.

10.45 to 11.0 a.m.—Demonstration by the 25th Fighter Squadron. Royal Air Force, by permission of Squadron Leader W. H. Park, M.C., D.F.C., commanding Royal Air Force Station, Hawkinge.

11.0 a.m.—His Royal Highness Prince Henry will arrive at the Borough Boundary in Cheriton Road, where he will be received by The Marquis Camden (Lord Lieutenant of Kent), who will present The Right Worshipful The Mayor (Alderman Reginald G. Wood, J.P.), The Recorder, Captain The Hon. E. B. S. Bingham, V.C., O.B.E., R.N., Squadron Leader W. H. Park, M.C., D.F.C., and the Town Clerk.

Proceed to the Town Hall via Cheriton Road, Castle Hill Avenue and Sandgate Road.

11.20 a.m.—Arrive at the Town Hall.

His Royal Highness will inspect the Guard of Honour from the 2nd Battalion South Staffordshire Regiment. In command, Captain J. M. Benoy.

Members of the Council will be presented to His Royal Highness in the Town Hall.

11.0 to 11.45 a.m.—Concert by the Municipal Orchestra in the Leas Cliff Hall, under the direction of Captain A. Holland, L.R.A.M.

11.30 a.m.—Members of the Council leave the Town Hall in motor cars for the Leas Cliff Hall.

11.40 a.m.—His Royal Highness accompanied by the Mayor, The Lord Lieutenant, The Recorder, Sir Philip Sassoon, Bart., C.M.G., M.P., The Marchioness Cholmondeley, Captain The Hon. E. B. S. Bingham, V.C., O.B.E., R.N., Colonel Commandant T. W. Stansfeld, C.M.G., D.S.O., Squadron Leader W. H. Park, M.C., D.F.C., and The Town Clerk, will leave the Town Hall for the Leas Cliff Hall via Sandgate Road, West Terrace and The Leas. At the War Memorial, His Royal Highness will place a wreath thereon and will inspect Members of the British Legion.

11.50 a.m.—Arrival of His Royal Highness at Leas Cliff Hall and inspection of Guard of Honour of the 234th (Howitzer Battery) R.A., T.A., Folkestone. In command, Major C. Bell.

12.0 noon.—The ceremony of declaring open the Leas Cliff Hall by His Royal Highness The Prince Henry.

The speeches of His Royal Highness and the Mayor will be broadcast throughout the British Isles, and the ceremony will be broadcast on The Leas and in the Marine Gardens Pavilion.

173. Items on the programme.

After the ceremony, His Royal Highness will leave the Leas Cliff Hall for the Hotel Metropole via The Leas, Clifton Crescent and The Leas, and enter the Hotel by the South Entrance.

1.0 p.m.—Luncheon to His Royal Highness at the Hotel Metropole.

2.20 p.m.—His Royal Highness will leave the Hotel Metropole for the Royal Victoria Hospital via Grimston Avenue, Shorncliffe Road, Castle Hill Avenue, Radnor Park Road and Radnor Park Avenue.

2.30 p.m.—His Royal Highness will declare open the new Extension of the Hospital.

2.50 p.m.—Leave the Hospital for the Harvey Grammar School via Radnor Park Avenue, Julian Road and Cheriton Road.

3.0 p.m.—Arrival at the Harvey Grammar School and inspection of Guard of Honour of 4th Battalion The Buffs, T.A., Folkestone. In command, Captain D. V. Coote.

His Royal Highness will lay the Foundation Stone of the proposed Extensions of the Harvey Grammar School.

3.15 to 4.15 p.m.—A Polo Match on the Polo Ground. 11th Hussars v. Crimson Ramblers.

Admission 1/-. Motor Cars 2/6 (additional).

3.30 p.m.—His Royal Highness will leave the Harvey Grammar School for the Polo Ground via Cherry Garden Avenue.

4.0 p.m.—Leave the Polo Ground by the main gates in Cheriton Road and proceed to the Royal Pavilion Hotel for Tea via Cheriton Road, Guildhall Street, Rendezvous Street and Tontine Street.

5.0 p.m.—Leave the Royal Pavilion Hotel for Lympne via Road of Remembrance, The Leas, Earl's Avenue and Sandgate Road to the Borough Boundary, where the Mayor will take leave of His Royal Highness, who will proceed to Lympne.

From **2.30** to **5.0** p.m. the Leas Cliff Hall will be open to the Public free for inspection.

At **5.30** p.m., Massed Drums, Fifes and Pipes will Beat the Retreat on the Leas near the Western end.

At **7.0** p.m., on the Sports Ground, Cheriton Road, there will be a Mounted Gymkhana, Historical and Musical Ride by the 11th Hussars, and Aerial Display by the kind permission of the Commanding Officer. Fireworks.

At **8.0** p.m., a Grand Concert in the Leas Cliff Hall for which Mr. Tom Burke, the famous Tenor, has been specially engaged.

174. On his way to the *Royal Pavilion Hotel* via Tontine Street and Harbour Street during the afternoon of his visit, Prince Henry passed the Folkestone lifeboat, the self-righting *Leslie*, launched in January 1904, which continued in service until 1930. Its coxswain was William Baker. Prince Henry is seen here in the rear passenger seat.

175. Seen here in 1928 is Folkestone Municipal Orchestra at its headquarters, the Leas Cliff Hall, which was opened the previous year. It was conducted by Eldrige Newman who remained Folkestone's Musical Director until 1939.

176. (*right*) One of the ways Folkestone attracted family visitors between the wars was by making a conscious effort to create flower-surrounded walks. There was active promotion of 'Floral Folkestone'. One idea was this zig-zag path, which was built so that those in bathchairs could be taken from the Leas at the top to the Lower Sandgate Road and the beach at the bottom. Flowers were planted either side of the route.

177. (*below*) Among other features established by the 'Floral Folkestone' theme between the wars was this special flower-bed outside the Leas Cliff Hall. Here it is marking the Silver Jubilee of King George V and Queen Mary in 1935.

178.   The Kingsnorth Gardens were created in 1928. The tower in the background is that of the United Reformed church, which in 1928 was the Congregational church. The gardens were once part of Ingles Farm. In 1847 John Kingsnorth, the tenant farmer, used the area as a clay pit for brick-making, the bricks being baked roughly where the *Park Inn Hotel*, formerly the *Central Hotel*, now is.

179.   Another facet of the 'Floral Folkestone' theme was an attempt to make attractive the area between the bottom of the cliffs and the Lower Sandgate Road. The programme seems to have been very successful.

Bibliography

Books

Bishop, Dr. C. H., *Folkestone, The Story of a Town* (1973)
Bishop, Dr. C. H., *Old Folkestone Pubs*
Bishop, Dr. C. H., *Some Folkestone Worthies*
Blaxland, Gregory, *South East Britain, Eternal Battleground* (1981)
Brown, Revd. J. H., *A History of the Harvey Grammar School* (1962)
Bushell, Peter, *Great Eccentrics* (1984)
Douch, John, *Smuggling – The Wicked Trade* (1980)
Fraser, Antonia, (Ed.), *The Lives of the Kings and Queens of England* (1975) ·
Forbes, Duncan, *Hythe Haven* (1982)
Glover, Judith, *The Place Names of Kent*, 2nd edn. (1982)
Hart, Brian, *Folkestone's Cliff Lifts* (1985)
Jessup, F. W., *A History of Kent* (1974)
Mackie, S. J., *Folkestone and its Neighbourhood and Gleanings from the Municipal Records* (1883)
Walton, John, *The English Seaside Resort* (1983)
Witney, K. P., *The Kingdom of Kent* (1982)

Local Guides and Monographs

Bishop, Dr. C. H., *Charles Dickens in Folkestone*
Boreham, Brian, *Martello Towers* (1986)
Edwards, Dame E., *St. Eanswythe of Folkestone* (1983)
Reader-Moore, A., *St. Mary and St. Eanswythe* (parish church guide, 1973)
Whitney, C. E., *Discovering the Cinque Ports* (1978)
Whitney, C. E., *The Visitor's Folkestone* (1984)

Articles

Davies, C. P., 'The Coming of the Railway', *Folkestone Past and Present* (1954)
Davies, C. P., 'A Glance at the Street Names', *Folkestone Past and Present* (1954)
Dickens, Charles, 'Out of Town', *Household Words* No. 288 (1855)
Grover, O. B., 'Tudor Folkestone', *Folkestone Past and Present* (1954)
Jones, L. R., 'Smuggling Days in Folkestone', *Folkestone Past and Present* (1954)
Pole Sturt, E., 'The History of Folkestone', *Folkestone Past and Present* (1954)

Miscellaneous

Folkestone Express
Kelly's Directory of Folkestone (1927-39)
Marrin, J. and P., *Folkestone 1790-1891, A Pictorial Catalogue of Engravings* (1984)
Morris, John, (Ed.), *Domesday Book: Kent* (1983)
Parson's Directory of Folkestone (1915, 1925)
Pike's Folkestone, Hythe and Sandgate Directory (1901-11)
The Times, various issues (1821-1914)